DANIEL WEBSTER JACKSON  & THE WRONGWAY RAILROAD

BY
ROBERT W. WALKER

Royal Fireworks Press
Unionville, New York

The author wishes to dedicate this book to the memory and spirit of Mark Twain.

Copyright © 2000, R Fireworks Publishing Company, Ltd.
All Rights Reserved.

Previously published in 1982 by Oak Tree Publications, San Diego, CA. This edition has been substantially revised.

Royal Fireworks Press
First Avenue, POB 399
Unionville, NY 10988-0399
(845) 726-4444
FAX: (845) 726-3824
EMAIL: rfpress@frontiernet.net

ISBN: 0-88092-554-X

Printed in the United States of America using vegetable-based inks on acid-free, recycled paper by the Royal Fireworks Printing Co. of Unionville, New York.

CHAPTER ONE

THE DEVIL'S ERRAND

NOVEMBER 17, 1852
HANNIBAL COUNTY, HANNIBAL, MISSOURI

The campfire lit the circle of boys, their eyes wide, as they listened to the storyteller. The flames rose and sank with a shifting wind that threw dry leaves into Old Black Billy's face. Old Billy stood over the circle, telling one of his famous "true" ghost stories. Behind the group stood black empty woods and the Negro quarters where most of the boys slept. Here and there among the black people, Daniel Webster Jackson and Joe Grier recognized a white face—other boys from town, who joined them in risking their skins to hear some of the old man's tales. Old Billy had a reputation in Hannibal.

The storyteller suddenly thrust his face toward Daniel's and howled with a blood curdling scream. "That was the cry Colonel Halverston heard when he got back to the place in the woods where them witches waited for him!" the old man said, pausing for a breath before adding, "Colonel man stared up into that big oak tree to find the witches, but colonel's horse reared up scared and throwed him off!" Old Billy jerked his hand upward to bring home his point, moving quickly around the circle.

From where Daniel sat, he could see the well-lit, four-story white house that belonged to the mysterious Colonel Halverston. It was an old mansion with large columns and great bay windows. Across the top floors, a line of windows offered a view of the land. The white walls looked green in darkness, thought Daniel, and he wondered if the colonel had really encountered witches in the nearby woods as a young man.

"It was a trap!" shouted one boy in the crowd.

"Can't trust devil-women!" cried another.

Old Billy kept his tale spinning, shouting over the listeners: "Colonel knew what he was about! He wanted to speak with Miss Amanda just once more, and the only way he could was by trusting in them witches! But Colonel, he protected himself with the riddle and his Bible, from which he took the riddle!"

A flurry of questions from Billy's anxious audience followed.

"What happened next?".

"What come of Miss Amanda?"

"Why didn't the colonel shoot 'em all?"

"There come giggling from up in that tree, them witches sounding just like school children, when one of them says to colonel smartlike, 'Why Colonel, you'll catch your death going about in your nightshirt on an evening cold as this!'" Again Billy paused for effect. "But Colonel, he stood up and said, 'Will I go back to my home and tell other men that the promises of a witch are false? For I will return and my tongue will be my own....'"

Suddenly, a large, black woman came up the embankment behind the storyteller and his audience. She came directly from the slave quarters, shouting, "Old Billy, you stop this here spook tale right now! You young'uns, get home!"

"What's the matter with you, Mattie?" asked Old Billy. "Can't you see we's all enjoying ourselves here?"

"Look up yonder, Billy." She pointed toward the big house. "Looks like the sheriff over to Hannibal's coming to hang you for your fool stories, old man."

Daniel saw torches and men descending the hill.

"My Lord, what could it be?" Old Billy wondered aloud.

"Colonel Halverston's done heard you clear from the house, telling that he's had doings with the Devil and witches, is what!" suggested Mattie as she took several children by the hand to start them homeward.

One boy, perhaps eleven, stopped to ask, "Are they going to sell you South, Mr. Billy?"

Old Billy grinned, tuffs of white hair lifting over his forehead. "Ain't likely, son. Go on with Mattie now."

"Better get them white boys home, too," Mattie called over her shoulder. "Them torches mean to get mad. They'll not take kindly to those white boys being out here."

But Daniel saw that Billy paid the boys no attention at all. Instead, Billy went to several men who had been sitting in the circle and whispered to them.

"Your colonel has joined them," one man shouted to Old Billy.

Daniel and Joe stared for a moment at one another, and then Joe pulled Daniel away, saying, "Let's get clear of here. My pap'll kill me if he learns I'm out here."

Daniel and Joe had only to take twenty paces to be completely hidden in the surrounding blackness. They rushed without running through the tall grass, careful not to stumble. "Come on, Daniel, we'll take the lower river trail."

But Daniel dropped to his knees. "Wait! Let's see what's up."

Joe crouched next to Daniel. "What are you doing?"

Daniel only crawled back toward the firelight filtering through the high grass. "Let's get out of here," urged Joe.

"Want to see what happens to Old Billy?"

"I ain't sure I do."

"Let's just see."

"Not me! I'm heading for town, Daniel. You get caught, you only have more chores. I get caught, my pap'll give me a walluping."

Daniel slowly looked over his shoulder. Joe was right there beside him, just as curious. Daniel was glad Joe hadn't run off and left him alone.

Colonel Halverston and Sheriff Brisbane from down at Hannibal, and a posse of sixteen tobacco-chewing Missourians, all carried long guns. The colonel and the sheriff argued loudly as they approached.

"A whole lot of slaves make it free, sheriff." Colonel Halverston sounded angry, his deep voice floated out over the tall grass where Daniel Webster Jackson and Joe Grier lay.

"You go about here shooting off your guns and running them noisy dogs up and down the Mississippi River and making like you catch all the runaways. You tell everybody in these parts only a scant few get away. You doctor all the numbers on the subject, you and the town council, because it doesn't look right on record that too many Negroes are running off, and it loses elections if too many are getting free! And your looking through the bush and my slave quarters every time a neighbor loses a slave he's mistreated is getting to be a mighty nuisance!"

"Beggin' the colonel's pardon sir, " began the sheriff. "You got no idea the nuisance me and my boys have been put through tonight. Five of 'em run off from Mr. Grimes' place over to Coleson County. Besides, you don't understand."

The colonel went right at the sheriff again, saying, "I understand this much: I look out my window, and I see you men here stretched across my land with torches. For all I know, it's a bunch of night riders, ready to set fire to my barn. You come in here unannounced, without a warrant, carrying guns!"

Below a leafless ash tree with a four-yard reach-around trunk, Sheriff Brisbane held up a hand now to the colonel when they stood before Old Billy. The tree's bark was shining from the torchlights held by the sixteen deputies.

"Colonel," began Sheriff Brisbane, his stomach barrel-round up to his chest was outlined against the night, "you just don't understand. Some folks been saying that more than not, they lose the trail of the runaways right in these parts, right here on your land! Oh, sure, I don't believe you got anything to do with it, but yonder's the Mississippi and yonder's Seaton woods, and beyond that the territories. Some folks think them runaways are disappearing right here! Now, I never believed a word of it, till tonight!"

"You think my man, Old Billy, and some of the others here are harboring runaways?" asked Colonel Halverston, staring up at the top of the tree.

"You know I do. I told you them Blacks just disappeared! Right over them hills there." He pointed toward the river.

"Get your search over with, sheriff," answered Colonel Halverston. He was a slender, tall and stiff-backed man who stood straighter than the tree beside him. "I'll tell you this much, sheriff, Judge Hatcher'll hear about this. You know what he thinks of such goings-on. He feels the same as I do about searching a man's home, invading and confiscating a man's property. You won't find a single man in those shacks who doesn't belong on this plantation."

"Colonel, sir, I ain't saying you'd harbor any slaves, nor steal any," pleaded Brisbane. "That's not what I'm saying."

"A man's got a right to privacy in this country, sheriff, even a black bondsman or slave, even Old Billly here—that's guaranteed by the Constitution of the United States, that's why we fought the Revolutionary War!"

"Revolution?" asked Sheriff Brisbane. "Oh, yeah. Well, I don't know nothing about history or the constitution. All I know is that the law tells me I got to run slaves if they run off! You heard of the Fugitive Slave Law, haven't you? Well, that tells me if Missouri's going to continue as a state, then we gotta honor our part of the bargain, and keep the slaves in the state."

"That's what the law says, does it?" asked the colonel.

"The way the law reads to me, it's all right we have a slave state same as Illinois has a free state, so long's we keep control on our slaves and don't have 'em running North and causing problems with the abolitionists!"

"Colonel talks like an abolition man to me," said one of the deputies at the sheriff's side. He ended by spitting tobacco juice onto the colonel's boot.

A long silence fell over the men while Colonel Halverston stared at the deputy. Then he walked up to the shabbily dressed man, who stood as tall as Halverston. With one swift movement, the colonel snatched off his white hat and slashed the man across the face with it. The deputy swung out with his fists, but Halverston stepped aside, grabbed the deputy's arm and pushed him right over.

"You watch your filthy tongue! Call me an abolitionist!" shouted Halverston.

Brisbane and the others looked at the colonel with respect, and no one helped the deputy off the ground.

"Search, sheriff!" the colonel ordered.

Old Billy stood beside the colonel, conferring in whispers. As the men began to search, the sheriff raised his hands while approaching the slave quarters. The sheriff continued his apologies for the benefit of several angry women who protested being roused from sleep. The black men stood in silence, dejected, turning their heads and eyes away from the white men with torches. The deputies went from man to man, searching each face with their roaring torchlight. The sheriff exclaimed, "Disappeared, whoof! Like smoke, I tell ya!"

At this, Old Billy rushed alongside the sheriff, saying, "Just like them tales I told you about, Master Brisbane, sir. You remember, about how the ground just opens up when a black man runs away? How I told you, how he stands there before this great big black hole that's come open in the dirt and staring out at him! And right then and there's when he may make free or be caught, 'cause he's given the choice."

"What's he talking about, sheriff?" asked the tobacco chewing deputy.

"Just foolishness, Lem," replied the sheriff.

"Ain't hardly foolish—it be the Devil's business," said Old Billy.

"Devil's business?" asked Lem.

"Like as not!" Billy answered with a wide grin. "How else you going to explain a thing like that? I mean disappearing like that?"

"Took my dog, Little Boy with 'em," complained the sheriff. "Sweetest little dog I ever owned. His first time out."

Lem added, "Little Boy was hot on their trail, too! No more'n half a mile from here. Swallowed up, them runaways were, along with Little Boy. Seen it with my own eyes, I did."

Old Billy had that look on his face that Daniel recognized—the same as just before he would end a story. Billy walked among the white men, shaking his head and saying, "Story has it that down in that big hole what swallows 'em up, they get to choose if they get caught or they go free."

"That's crazy," said another deputy, "how?"

"Devil has 'em sign over a paper. Makes 'em his slaves. They've got to sell their souls to make free in this world—woe to them! There they be slaves all over again—Satan's slaves!"

"Then the Devil's a gawl-dern abolitionist," said Lem, astonished at the thought.

"Hmmmpf!" The sheriff shook his head and waved off Billy's notion, disbelieving.

Some of the deputies got together and mulled it over. One of them went to Lem, who spoke up: "Wait a minute, Billy. That don't take into account them who make it free and are caught up North and brought back."

Old Billy only shrugged. "There're some who think they can outsmart even Satan! They sign another man's mark. But the Old Gent gets 'em in the end anyhow!"

"Listen to this," Daniel whispered to Joe in their hiding place, "that last line of Old Billy's is the grabber."

"What?" asked Joe.

"Old Billy, he just caught up the sheriff's men with a real whopper of an end to his tale."

Joe nodded now, understanding. "We'd best get outta here before we're mistook for them runaways and shot down."

Daniel and Joe crawled along the ground on their bellies. Somewhere they became separated, and Daniel stood up to have a look around. Suddenly, he was yanked to the ground and a hand covered his mouth. He was unsure who had hold of him; he knew it couldn't be Joe Grier. The man whispered in a hoarse voice, "Don't yell out, boy!" Daniel felt the large, black man's sweat as it dripped onto his. "I got a knife, and if you so much as make a sound, I'll cut your heart out."

Daniel began to sweat more. He had a vague sense that a dog came alongside them, panting and patient, but he could not see. He wondered if he'd be alive for the new year of 1853. It was November. He was fifteen. His heart was pounding. He continued sweating even as he felt the powerful arm loosen its grip on him. The night wind chilled him as it whined through the blades of tall grass where they lay.

"Are you...one of them—them runaways from over...to Coleson County?" Daniel stuttered.

"Shhh, boy!"

Daniel decided the man was one of the Coleson runaways and that he'd best do as told. He lay there and eyed the black man, who couldn't be more than twenty years old himself. The runaway watched the deputies observing every face, every detail. Daniel studied the runaway's features. He seemed to be short but bull-shouldered, with arms so thick and powerful as to resemble tree limbs. His round face shone in the moonlight, covered with sweat. A tuft of mustache sat beneath flaring nostrils. He had a high forehead, the man's cheekbones showed prominently below his white-yellow eyes. His hair, thick and curled as wire, looked rust-colored in the dark.

"You're one of them runaways they're chasing, aren't you?"

The black man stared again into Daniel's face. "You gotta lot of nerve. I tol' you to shut up." He showed Daniel the knife, a ten-inch blade extending from the hilt, and he placed it again at Daniel's throat. The boy swallowed, which made the blade tickle his Adam's apple.

"Keep yourself still as a rock, and you won't get hurt," hissed the stranger. "Don't move, don't speak no more."

Daniel did as told.

Resting his long gun against the tree under which the men had earlier stood, Sheriff Brisbane was making apologies to Colonel Halverston. Daniel could barely hear their talk now, but then the sheriff shouted, "We'll take out yonder way, men." The next moment men and dogs headed right for Daniel and the runaway, and Daniel felt the vice-like grip of the stranger tighten on his wrists. Rising only to a crouching position, he pulled Daniel along toward the slave quarters. Again a dog ran with them, and Daniel wondered aloud, "Is that Sheriff Brisbane's dog?"

"Quiet!" came the reply, and again, they ducked below the tall grass, breathing hard.

"Down!" whispered the runaway, shoving Daniel's face onto the ground and lying over him, almost suffocating him.

To his left, from out of the corner of his eye, Daniel saw the grass moving. He heard the posse pass close by. Then he felt the relief in the man who lay over him. The big man spoke, after another minute, as if to himself, "I shoulda took my chance with the Devil. I shoulda stayed with the others and gone down in that hole."

"Can I get up?" asked Daniel.

"Yes, but stay low, boy."

"Whataya mean when you say the others went down in the hole, and you shoulda taken your chances with the Devil?" asked Daniel.

"I ain't never seen nothing like it," began the man, shaking his head. "Ground just cracked open, and all of us yelled and scattered. But up pops someone from the hole and says, 'This-a-way!' and the others rushed right in there, more a-feared of the dogs than the Devil, I guess. But me, I was too scared! I couldn't! I couldn't let Satan have me. I take slavery before I take the Devil!"

Daniel shook his head over this, unsure what to say or believe. He had heard Old Billy's tale, but he'd taken it to be just another of his stories. Yet, here sat a man who'd seen the hole and the slaves go in and not return. Satan had even spoken to him!

Daniel looked up to where Old Billy still stood beneath the ash tree. He saw two black men climb down from the tree. Surprised, he watched intently. Colonel Halverston waved Old Billy off, and he now stood halfway between the slave quarters and the house. *Does the colonel see these newcomers too?* Daniel recalled how, earlier, the colonel had stared directly up the very tree in which these men had been hiding. *If they were in the tree, hiding from the sheriff, they must be runaways, and if they are runaways, why didn't the colonel pointed them out? How could the colonel have missed seeing them?*

Confused, Daniel turned back to the big man beside him. Both the stranger and the dog were gone.

⧖ ⧖ ⧖

"Where in tarnation you been?" asked Joe when Daniel reached the river road where Joe'd waited for him.

Daniel felt unsure whether he ought to tell Joe about the runaway. Joe's feelings about slaves ran high, depending on what his pap told him. His pap's views depended on whether he was drunk or sober. Joe believed no man knew more about life than his pap, drunk or sober.

"Got lost and turned around in the grass," replied Daniel. "It all looks the same, you know."

"Lost?" Joe said with a laugh. "You?"

"You know, like when you can't find your way," Daniel answered and quickly changed the subject. "Look here, you ever hear of that hole before?"

"What hole?" Joe was all of two years older than Daniel.

"The hole Old Billy told the sheriff and his men all about."

"Oh, you mean the yarn!"

"You ever hear tell of it before?"

"Sure, I heard it lots of times. Just never paid it no mind."

"Where else ya hear of that hole?"

"Heard my pap talking 'bout it once to some men. But black folks mostly tells about it."

"Do you believe it?" asked Daniel.

"Pay it as much mind as any of Old Billy's ghost and goblin stories."

"Don't you believe any of Old Billy's tales?"

"Sure," replied Joe, "some of 'em. The ones with real names, real dates and real places."

"Why'd you believe them?"

"They can be proved—*authenticated,* my pap says."

Daniel looked at Joe's chain around his neck with the metal charm dangling there. It was a good luck charm Joe had bought back from Old Billy. After selling it, Joe'd had a run of awful luck. Then be bought it back. Maybe Joe was the wrong person to have this talk with, Daniel decided. Besides, they'd be parting in a few minutes, having reached Hannibal. *What would Joe say if I told him about the runaway?* he wondered.

Joe lived in shantytown, along the north stretch of river leading into town. Prospectors, trappers, traders and traveling folk on their way to the territories camped like a band of gypsies. Nine months of the year fathers took out for the territories to hunt for bison, furs or gold. The other three months, men like Joe's pap, who'd returned beaten and tired, spent their time drinking and telling stories of their adventures in the wilderness. You couldn't tell Joe that it would be safer to believe Old Billy's tales. He'd fight you, sure you were calling his pap a liar.

"You ever wonder what becomes of those runaways who never get found?" Daniel finally asked.

"No."

"Ain't you even curious?"

"Don't know why they run away in the first place," Joe answered, thinking hard. "Pap don't even know. He says it must be something in their blood. Maybe the same thing that makes 'em black and don't make us black-skinned, as pap says."

Daniel did not answer. He stood still and tried to understand what Joe and just said.

"But if pap don't understand it, a grown up man like him, fought in the Mexico war and all, then how you think we can ever understand it?"

Daniel only frowned while Joe went on talking. "Pap says it ain't smart to try to figure out what a black man is thinking. He says he knows folks who've gone crazy trying to understand 'em. He thinks Colonel Halverston is that way."

They reached the fork in the dusty road which led to shantytown, and Joe ran off, turning once to wave to Daniel. Daniel looked ahead up the town road where some few lights hung out over the harbor. Boats and barges were tied-to for the night. He dreaded going home to his cramped room out back of Mrs. Shorr's. Mrs. Shorr boarded as many wards of the court and orphans as she could find or make room for on her floors and in her sheds. For each child she boarded, Judge Hatcher saw to it the town paid her properly. Daniel did not know how much Mrs. Shorr got for each of her "children" as she called them, but he did know that in the bargain, she gained a houseful of window washers, gardeners, painters, menders, fishermen, hog-sloppers, hunters, knitters, butter churners, wheel spinners, and wood choppers. For his trouble, Daniel gained a straw-tick mattress in a lean-to which he shared with three other of Mrs. Shorr's unfortunate children. The lucky boys and girls who lived in the house ate better and were generally treated better, Mrs. Shorr having long before established her system of rewards and punishments.

The lean-to, a crumbling, aged shack that had been built onto the freshly white-washed main house, came into Daniel's view. As he approached, he shook his head over the sad sight. The old palace, he called it. It would fall in one day, he told himself. Daniel saw that the lights remained out, and everything felt silent and still. He would have no trouble slipping back into his bed.

He'd lived with Mrs. Shorr for nine years, since he was six, the year his parents caught the fever and died. He thought about his parents now and why they had first traveled to Hannibal. The Jacksons had traded all the way from a place called Hartford in Connecticut, following the Ohio River to St. Louis, Missouri, where they purchased a new wagon and more trading goods. They had intended to trade their way to California. But they stopped in Hannibal in search of Daniel's maternal uncle who'd come ahead of them.

One day a couple years back after Daniel asked around, Old Billy took him aside and told him about his father and mother. Old Billy said he never saw any man handle a team of horses the way Daniel's pap had, the day he'd thundered down Main Street with Daniel's mother beside him. The wagon, heavy with a load of chairs, trunks, dishpans, pots, ladles, spoons, gourds, tins, saucers and cups, threatened to collapse.

Samuel Todd Jackson had been his name. He stood six foot four and had eyes of a hazelnut brown. He'd quit drinking at age nineteen and became a trader, a traveling tinkerman, to make his way to the Pacific Ocean. Lean and tall, Sam Jackson was handsome when he laughed, Old Billy said, "And your pap laughed all the time."

Daniel's mother, Carrie Webster, was a pretty, small woman with long hair, the color of cornsilk. Billy told Daniel that his mother had been strong and brave. She wanted to go West as much as her husband. Together, Daniel's parents had put in to Hannibal for a brother of hers who was no longer there, to take on more supplies, and to do some trading. But it proved a bad year all around, and they had to stay on for a time. When the sickness came to Hannibal that year, she'd gone from house to house to help out any way she could. The fever took them both.

Just as Daniel reached the door, Mrs. Shorr, with a broomstick in her hand, jumped out at him. He thought immediately of Old Billy's story of the witches in Seaton woods. "Oh, Mrs. Shorr! I thought you was a witch!"

"Witch, I'll give you witch! You'll wish I was just a witch!" She began, thrashing at him with the broom.

"Where you been, boy? What Devil's nest you been in this time o'night? Answer!"

Hit several times by the broom, Daniel reached out and snatched it from the old woman's hands. Mrs. Shorr, a thin-faced, wizened woman, looked as stiff as the clothes on her line left in the frost. She threw up her skinny arms shouting, "You going to attack? You Devil boy! Come ahead! I'm man enough to knock you over, you whelp!"

At the doorway to the lean-to stood Jeremy Small and Tad Burroughs, Jeremiah and Thaddeus, as Mrs. Shorr called the boys, in the same nasal way she would call him Daniel Webster. Tad and Jeremy, several years younger than Daniel, stared out at the broom battle going on. Daniel felt sorry for their little hungry bodies, their fears, and their position in the lean-to, with Mrs. Shorr squeezing their childhood from them. *Too bad they've been placed with her,* he thought. *And I'm as trapped as they are.* He dropped the broom at his feet, stared into Mrs. Shorr's steely gray eyes and went into the lean-to without another word. Mrs. Shorr's remarks sailed over the heads of the other children at the doorway.

"I'll just see about you tomorrow, Daniel Webster! I'll just see to you. Mark my word, I will! Judge Hatcher'll hear of this. I've got enough to worry my soul without you out in the night over to those Negro quarters, getting into who knows what sort of trouble! Tampering with them voodoo ways of theirs!"

She lashed out at Tad and Jeremy, pushed them into the lean-to, and closed the door, leaving all of her court-appointed charges in the dakrness.

CHAPTER TWO

THE JUDGE'S SPY

"After all the poor woman's done for you, Daniel," intoned Judge Hatcher. "How can you go on disobeying her and hurting her—raising a rake to her!"

"It were a broom, and she raised it to me," answered Daniel, trembling before the judge's desk in the middle of the clapboard courthouse.

"She can hit you all she wants, son. She's got your best interest at heart. She's got to raise you up a proper, respectful citizen. She doesn't have to do it, she just does!"

Judge Hatcher allowed this to sink in before he climbed from his wooden chair and stepped around the desk to stand over Daniel. "You ought to be proper ashamed of yourself, sassing Mrs. Shorr, taking her broom from her, and chasing her with a rake."

Daniel dropped his head and stared at his feet.

"She tells me you been sneaking off. Now, son, are you going to tell me where you got off to last night?"

"No place particular," he replied.

"Mrs. Shorr thinks you were on some Devil's errand, son. Now out with it!"

"Just walked over to Colonel Halverston's at the slave quarters is all."

The judge leaned in closer, his jaw drooping as he said, "Halverston's place? Really? Mrs. Shorr didn't say it was to Halverston's you've been going." The judge stroked his hairless chin as if pulling on an invisible beard. He paced and next he let out a thin-sounding, "Hmmm...."

"Mayn't I be going now, sir?" asked Daniel, head still hanging, eyes fixed on the floor. He watched as the judge's shoes came in and out of his sight, the wood floor squeaking as the shoes went over loose boards.

Instead of answering, the judge began sizing Daniel up like a hefer or a hog at the Hannibal Founder's Day Fair.

"Mrs. Shorr, she's sore angry with me," Daniel shakily began, "and she lay out twelve, maybe thirteen days worth of chores, and she won't never let me take time from her school to do the work, so I—"

Suddenly, Judge Hatcher erupted with words, saying, "Why do you go out there, Daniel? To Halverston's quarters?"

"Don't rightly know. Fun maybe?"

The judge hummed through his teeth, thinking deeper thoughts, when again he erupted. "Why, it's Old Billy, ain't it?"

"Old Billy, sir?"

"Your taken with Old Black Billy's wild yarns and ghosts stories. Is that right?" He didn't wait for Daniel's answer. "You'll never get nowhere in this life sitting and listening to foolish stories of witches and ghouls told by an old man, son."

"But Old Billy tells some stories that are true," Daniel defended Old Billy.

"True? Old Billy and the word *true* don't even run together, son. Billy never stops himself to ask which is true and which is made up."

"What about the story he told me about my mam and my pap? It's got names and dates and places–things you may au-au-auth-thin-icate."

The judge considered this a moment. "I reckon the one he tells about your folks is close enough to the truth."

Daniel breathed in relief, while Judge Hatcher started down another path, asking, "You ever see anything unusual out there at the colonel's place, son?"

Giving thought to the two slaves who'd shinnied down the thick ash, and the one who'd held a gutting knife to his throat, Daniel wondered if he dared say a word. He feared Old Billy could be harmed by what he told. "Unusual?" he finally asked.

"Unusual, strange goings-on, anything out of the ordinary? Any strangers thereabouts?" The questions now poured floodlike from the judge, his eyes wide.

"Not any so's I'd notice."

"What does that mean?" Hatcher asked.

"I haven't seen no strangeers that I know out that way, sir," replied Daniel.

Exasperated, his hands on his head now, the judge said, "Daniel, if they're strangers, of course you aren't going to know any of 'em."

"That's what I said; wasn't that what I said?" Daniel didn't wish to lie to Judge Hatcher, not if he could help it, but he didn't want Billy fetching any trouble either. Still, Judge Hatcher stood for the law hereabouts. He stood for the rules, and Daniel knew a smart body didn't lie to a lawman.

"I'm going to ask you once more, Daniel. Did you ever see anyone—white, black, green, I don't care what color—anyone who did not belong out at Halverston's? Anything come to mind?" The judge's round belly heaved now, his voice thick. "Did you meet anyone there, for instance, who Old Billy introduced around as his long lost cousin or uncle or brother or sister? Anything like that?"

"No sir, no cousins or other relatives."

Daniel knew that Sheriff Brisbane, whose office opened on this one, had already reported to Hatcher on what had happened at Halverston's, how they had lost the chase and the sheriff's dog to a mystery. By saying nothing, at least he'd keep the sheriff out of trouble, as well as Old Billy. Still, Daniel's head felt mixed up, unsure what to do. If the judge found out later that he withheld information, he might be arrested for aiding and abetting fugitive slaves. Locked up as an abolitionist, Daniel'd never be able to face anyone in Hannibal ever again.

The judge leaned his large frame against his desk, picked up a sheet of paper and fanned himself. While he was not as large around as the sheriff, Judge Hatcher seemed always to be sweating.

The judge shot out a question like buckshot from a scatter gun. "You ever hear Old Billy or any of them black folk of Halverston's tell about a hole, a great big hole that opens up out there? One that swallows up runaways and dogs whole?"

Daniel was afraid to say yes and afraid to say no. "No, sir, I ain't never heard of it, not while Old Billy was telling stories last night." It wasn't quite a lie. Old Billy didn't say it while he was telling stories. He'd said it when the sheriff began his search. "And, I ain't never seen nor heard nothing unusual out at Colonel Halverston's."

The judge began to pace again. The wood flooring again squeaked under his weight. The judge was as tall as Colonel Halverston. His face was largely made up of a big jaw, extending way out beyond his neck, in a hang-dog, angry fashion lately. He now spoke as if to himself now. "I don't like that Halverston. Elections coming up, and he's after my job."

Just then Sheriff Brisbane arrived. "Wanted to see me?"

"No," answered the judge. Then he raised his hands and approached the sheriff, contradicting himself. "I mean, yes. But, I got a different plan now."

"A different plan?" asked the sheriff.

"Come over here, Henry," the judge said as he guided the sheriff to where Daniel stood. "Here's my new plan." He pointed right at Daniel.

The sheriff stared at Daniel Webster Jackson, unimpressed. "This here is young Webster Jackson, ain't it?"

"Young Daniel here is going to help me win this election."

"Why, there ain't no reason to worry about this election, judge. I told you, nobody's going to vote for the colonel. He's too new to these parts."

"He's been here for seven years, Henry."

"But he wasn't born here, judge. He ain't even Missouri-born."

"I come from Virginia myself, Henry." "And he's a colonel in the U.S. Cavlary," moaned the judge.

"Was, judge. *Was* a colonel."

"Everyone still calls him colonel. He calls himself colonel. He's stumping as colonel. And I hear talk, Henry, talk that'll put you and me out of business."

"West Point colonel, fought in the Mexico War," said Brisbane, who was still not impressed. "Resigned his commission, judge. You got that!"

"All you know is he resigned his commission," sniffed the judge. "You don't know why. Why?"

"I told you, nobody knows why. He just up and did it. Just say it was cowardice."

"He hardly strikes me as a coward."

"He don't have to strike you as a coward. We just have to spread the rumor and let people think what they will."

"You wouldn't do that, would you, judge?" asked Daniel.

The sheriff and the judge looked at Daniel at the same moment with the same intensity in their eyes.

"No," began the sheriff. "Nobody'd do that."

Judge Hatcher put up a hand for the sheriff to stop talking, and he put his arm around Daniel's shoulder and led him to a corner.

"Daniel, you do want to help me, don't you? I've always done right by you, you know that. I wouldn't lie, cheat, or steal anything, including one vote from an honest man, but this here colonel's not an honest man. He's going around telling tales about the sheriff and me—lies, just so he can get elected."

"Lies?" repeated Daniel.

"You know what the Good Book says about an eye for an eye; well, in this case it's a lie for a lie."

"Then you're calling yourself a liar, judge?"

"No, no! Don't mean I'm a liar, not during an election. Elections are run that way. The colonel's getting folks all worked up over the number of runaway slaves that've gotten free. Says he can do better! See to it they are stopped! He even has a head count on the number of slaves reported run away and never caught! Says he's kept it since he moved into these parts seven years ago—phony figures, more lies! It's plain to see he's been planning this all along. Just when the iron's hot, he goes to make his play for my job."

The sheriff listened in on the judge's words, and joining them, he said, "We've done all we can, judge. I mean, I've raided his place so many times I found our footprints still there from the last time! And we found nothing! For the life of me, I can't see why any man would risk life in prison or a hanging just so he can have your job...ahhh, sir."

"He's got the notion we're making off with the town treasury, Henry, and he thinks he can do better running Hannibal." The judge shook his head in disbelief. "I give up my life for this godforsaken place, and what do I get in return? Lowdown accusations."

The sheriff placed a hand on Judge Hatcher's shoulder and said, "If we could only find out just how them runaways disappear on us out yonder."

"We're going to," stated the judge. "With young Daniel's help, we're going to learn precisely what sort of magician's trick is going on out there."

"What?" asked Daniel.

"How's this pup going to do what me and my boys couldn't?"

The judge stepped back around his desk, fell into his hard wood chair and grinned. "Color of his skin."

Brisbane asked, "What of it?"

"Look at how tarnished copper this boy is. With a little lampblack over his skin, maybe some tar and tobacco, we'll have us our own spy on the inside." The judge then spoke directly to Daniel, asking, "How'd you like to take your orders from me instead of that mean old Mrs. Shorr, Daniel? I know you don't want to disappoint me, do you, boy?"

"Spy? But I got all them chores to do, enough for weeks."

"I'll see to that."

"But I don't know anything about being a spy."

"I'll teach you all there is to it."

Daniel had never disobeyed the judge, and he'd always trusted him. Now, his head spinning, he didn't know what to say or do to get out of this strange request. "Spy?" he kept saying. "Me, a spy?"

⌛ ⌛ ⌛

Spy, spy, spy, Daniel kept saying over in his head. "I'd as likely be a doctor as a spy, judge."

But the judge didn't hear, deep in conversation with the sheriff. The two of them now leaned over the desk at one another. Brisbane thought using a fifteen-year-old boy as a spy was a mad idea.

"If you'd caught them runaways like you were supposed to, I wouldn't have to resort to such skulduggery, Henry," protested the judge.

"I do catch runaways, all the time! Got one last night, even."

"Oh, yes. What'd you find out from him?'

"Nothing, 'cept maybe he's crazy and that's why he run off in the first place—but smart crazy, this one is."

"Smart crazy?"

"You know what I mean. Crazy enough to tell a tale so far from the truth, well...it takes you by surprise, so you almost want to believe it."

"What kind of story?"

Daniel tried to interrupt, saying, "You caught one of the Coleson County runaways last night?"

The sheriff went on, saying, "Something crazy about his being a bounty hunter himself." Brisbane laughed at the notion. "Says he was hired by someone to chase down runaways himself! Can you beat that, judge?"

The judge sat thinking and muttering, "If it's true, even a little bit...."

"Then he'd be the lowest down man on earth, I reckon," said the sheriff.

"Who'd he say hired him?" asked Hatcher.

"I don't know. Showed me papers, all signed and printed with a big State of Illinois seal on 'em, but he didn't fool me."

"Had the State Seal on it?"

"Forgery, I figure, judge."

"One smart Negro if he's forged the State Seal."

"Seems to think highly of hisself, judge. Was carrying a long gun and a skinning knife when we caught him. Had a dog with him, too, but it wasn't the one I lost."

"You examined the papers he had? Were they a bill of sale on himself?"

"Reckon so, but like I said, I took it for a fake."

"Where are the papers now?"

"I tore 'em to shreds and threw 'em in his face, judge."

"Did you even bother to read the names on the document?"

Brisbane dropped his gaze and his voice, replying, "You know I don't read so well, judge."

"Better go have a talk with this fella myself," finished the judge, fighting again to his feet, and going for the cells.

But the sheriff stopped him with a question. "Mayn't I keep the dog, judge? Like I told you, I lost mine last night."

"Depends on our man. If he cooperates, we may have to return his dog to him. If he helps us, we can help him. He's in an awful fix, running away, and with a rifle in his hand."

Daniel, left standing in the middle of the courtroom, wondered which of the runaways had been captured. He wondered if it could be the man who'd held him on the ground at knife point. He felt sorry for the man, whoever he was. It could go bad for a runaway. Generally, they were sold South where it was said they'd be worked to death in the sugarcane fields. Daniel also wondered what the judge wanted from him, what he expected from him. "I ain't no spy," he told the empty room. He was supposed to look out for anything unusual at the colonel's, for a "hole" in the earth for runaways, and for an underground passage, an under-the-ground railroad! He'd only seen one regular railroad train in his life, two years before in St. Louis. *How am I going to get out of this?* he asked himself. *Why didn't I stay home the other night? Why didn't I pay Mrs. Shorr's rules more mind?*

CHAPTER THREE

THE NIGHT VISITOR

Climbing Cardiff Hill in the dark was not as hard as fighting back the feeling that he'd made a terrible mistake and should return to Hannibal, give himself up and confess everything to Judge Hatcher.

Wind whipped around Daniel, swirling dust and leaves into his face. He felt cold, and it smelled like rain coming. He felt more numb than hurt when he scratched his arm or hand on a branch as he made his way to the cave entrance only he and Joe knew about. Maybe the worst thing he'd done was wait too long to make up his mind about running away. He'd stopped at Joe's house and tried hard to talk Joe into running away, too. They argued because Joe didn't see any use in going, and he couldn't understand why Daniel wanted to leave. Although Joe had always talked about going West to the territories, even bragged about it, now he had a change of heart.

Cardiff was a rocky hill; sand and pine cones nestled comfortably in pitted holes, and stones covered much of the ground like so many apples tossed away. The steep hill proved treacherous here, overlooking the ribbon of the Mississippi River. Sycamores, sumacs, oaks, and ash trees grew on the hillside, with an occasional bramble bush that grabbed at Daniel as he went. Hills along the river like this one were dotted with caves and enclaves. The cave Daniel searched for had been a lot easier to find by day.

At the cave mouth there would be a lot of brush and brambles. He and Joe had moved it there to keep their cave a secret. Now, in the dark, every bush he saw looked to be covering a cave.

Then he spotted the right one, knowing the brush about the rock wall didn't look regular. He snatched away the covering. Met with the black interior, he told himself, *At least I'll be out of the cold wind and the wet.* A light shower had just begun.

He carried in all of the branches his arms could hold. There'd be more stored neatly on a ledge inside. Soon he had a small fire blazing. The cave openning was a lantern to anyone passing by, but it faced the river, and there wouldn't be any traffic on the water, not tonight, not with a storm coming.

Daniel stretched out beside the fire, and despite his worries, he fell asleep. Daniel slept with his arms wrapped about himself. Cool, rain-swept air filled the cave with a damp smell; one of fallen leaves, brown grass, and rotten stumps all mixed up with the river down the hill.

The sound of the rain had put Daniel to sleep. Something else woke him, wondering what it could be. *A dream,* he thought, listening for it again.

"Hooooooowl!" came a moaning from the woods beyond. "Hooooooowl!"

Man or animal? Daniel wondered, trying to identify the sound as it mixed with the howl of wind and rain. He crept to the cave mouth, afraid, unsure. He heard twigs snapping. Someone—or something—was coming his way. He glanced over his shoulder to the deep interior of the cave. He and Joe had never gone too far inside the cave, because at one point it narrowed so badly they would have had to lie down, slide and squeeze ahead—without any promise of ever being able to get back out. *Tonight I might have to risk it, unless maybe it's Joe out there.* He felt somewhat braver. "Joe? Is that you out there?" he called over the rain.

Only the heavy drumming of the rain answered. *If it isn't Joe out there, then I've just given away the secret of my hiding place.* He pictured the posse of sixteen torch-bearing men led by Sheriff Brisbane storming up the hill, angry, looking to kill him for disobeying the judge, and for making them come out on a night like this. He waited and waited, but no one came. He sat, looking into the fire.

Maybe it had been an owl or a passing bear. He hoped for an owl. A bear could be dangerous. He inched back to the front of the cave and looked out. There was a strange light, far away, on the Illinois side of the river, way up on a hill, at about the same height as Cardiff Hill. The light glowed like a fire, but it blinked on and off, like a signal! Someone seemed to be sending signals from Illinois, clear across the river!

Daniel stepped out farther toward the rock ledge, which stretched out over the river. It formed a natural roof over the alcove below him. Then he saw a flatboat barely a mile offshore, trying to make it across the river, fighting a headwind and pelting rain. Daniel wouldn't have seen the flatboat at all if a light had not been placed close to its rudder, and lit that very moment. In another second, the light went out.

It was no small skiff, rather a large affair, the kind of boat whole river families lived on and traded from. Daniel had heard stories of men and women whose entire lives were spent on such flatboats; born on them, raised to full age, and died on them without ever coming ashore. Old Billy once told him that some of the river folk never had any reason to come ashore and would get the giddies just like a cow if they stepped on dry land. These trading vessels traveled up and down the river with everything a man owned, with goats, chickens, dogs, children, and family covering every inch of deck. Some of the boats were fitted around with fences to hold the animals in. Shacks with stovepipes and dark little windows sat atop the flat-bottomed deck as well.

Daniel had never before seen one of these traveling in the dark. He'd never heard of anyone so ignorant as to try to make a river crossing in a storm. Even the ferryman at Harpers Crossing wouldn't do that. Everyone knew it was a fool's game to chance night travel in rough weather, because a good wave could take a goat, a cow or a child overboard. Besides, there was the danger of being run down by a steamer. *It's a wonder these people aren't tied up somewhere tonight,* Daniel thought. *An experienced raftsman would cuss them good for such foolishness.*

Daniel rushed back into the cave. The rain had become heavy again. At the cave entrance, he stopped, feeling his heart racing in his chest. A dog sat warming himself by the fire. He was a handsome, trim black and tan hunting dog. *Could this be the sheriff's lost dog, Little Boy?*

The dog stared at the fire, more interested in its warmth than in Daniel. "Got no fear of people, have you?" asked

Daniel. "If you ain't Little Boy, then maybe you belong to a farm nearby, huh?"

Daniel cautiously approached the dog, his fingers stretched out. "I ain't got nothing to eat, but you're welcome to my fire and my cave."

But just as Daniel reached out to pet him, the dog dodged his hand, backing into a darkened corner where he slumped down. "It's okay, boy, " Daniel said, "I ain't going to hurt you." Daniel decided to let the dog lay where he felt comfortable. "Glad to have the company," he added as he nestled near the fire himself. "I'm certain to run into some cutthroats, thieves and liars where I'm heading. Folks tell me Indian Territory is full up with pirates and murderers. Lighting out for the territories, I reckon. Nothing to keep me here, nothing to recommend my staying."

Daniel noticed that the dog was not only a handsome hunting dog, but a good listener as well. The rain had soaked the poor dog, and he continued panting as if he'd been running hard. But there had been no one outside. He wondered who the dog belonged to and where he'd come from.

Daniel threw a large branch of hickory on the fire, laid back down and tried to get the dog and Judge Hatcher off his mind. He wrapped his arms about hmself and closed his eyes...never once having seen the dark man in deep shadow behind the dog. The man's sharp eyes never left Daniel. He'd listened to every word Daniel had said and how he said it. Seeing Daniel nod off to sleep, he also closed his eyes, sitting cross-legged on the cave floor.

CHAPTER FOUR

THE RUNAWAY CATCHER

Daniel Webster Jackson felt his eyelashes curling under a force of hot air, as if he had rolled too close to the fire, and he heard a heavy breathing in his ear. His senses told him that morning had come. He smelled the sun on the cool, wet leaves just outside the cave. Then he realized someone's weight over his chest had made him instinctively draw up his legs and arms. He still held his eyes tightly closed. A bear, he feared, had come into the cave and now hovered over him, ready to pounce.

He lay for a few moments as still as stone. He heard the cock crow away off in Hannibal, and the rhythm of the river below, lapping in and out at the shore. The river must surely be swelled high with night rain to be cutting sand and rock with such energy this time of morning.

Daniel feared he'd be eaten alive if he dared show any sign of life. He dared not open his eyes. Instead, he concentrated on the faint sound of a bell ringing back in town. *Mrs. Shorr's school bell.* Mrs. Shorr also schooled Hannibal's children, and with her speller in her left hand, she rang the bell the way a boy swung a dead cat by its tail. Daniel imagined her now, and all the children racing for school, some of the boys lagging behind. He wished ever so much to be there now, though he'd never had any use for it before. Daniel began a silent prayer, swearing he'd never again smoke a pipe, skip school, play cards with the boys or slip away from Mrs. Shorr's ever again if he should live through the bear attack.

Then the animal thing standing over Daniel, straddling him, barked pertly and lapped at Daniel's face with a rough tongue. *The dog!* Daniel recalled his night visitor now. Daniel pushed the dog off, saying, "Hey, cut it out!"

When Daniel got free, he sized the dog up. A good-looking dog, his black dotted eyebrows looked deep and dark against his tan hide. The forehead jutted forward, regal and high. The dog moved his head from side to side, tilting it, studying Daniel as Daniel studied him. "Does your tail ever stop wagging?" Daniel asked.

The dog barked loudly in response and placed a paw out for Daniel to shake, but as Daniel attempted a shake, the dog drew back. He didn't want to be touched. Instead, he stiffened, his tail going straight back as if he were on the scent. *He moves like a stern-wheeler when it slows and reverses in mid-river to make a landing,* Daniel thought.

Suddenly, the dog growled at Daniel, freezing him in place.

"Hush dog! Stand away!" a man's clear voice rang out. For a moment, Daniel thought the words had come from the dog, but then he saw the movement in the shadows at the rear of the cave. *The man came in with the dog and was here all night. He's as agile as his dog.* Daniel's hand went instinctively to his throat. *At least he didn't slit my throat in the night.*

Daniel leapt to his feet, aiming for the sunlit exit, but the dog blocked his way, snarling and mean now. The shadow man calmly said, "My dog'll eat you alive, boy. He's a mean'un, kept hungry all the time, and he does like I tells him. Samuel, heel!"

The dog immediately relaxed.

Daniel gulped and turned his eyes on the man crouched in the shadows, his large form nearly invisible against the cave wall even by day.

"My dog Samuel is trained on runaways, and we're right now looking for some who stole off from over at Coleson County, belong to a Mr. James Grimes. Mr. Grimes put great store on his people; put a heavy price tag on 'em, too. Come this way maybe just last evening? You hear tell of 'em?"

"No...I'm new to these parts myself," Daniel lied.

"Sam and me was hunting these slaves and doing fine till the other night. Then this fool sheriff and his posse caught me and Sam. Said we was runaways! Locked me up down at Hannibal. You ever been to Hannibal? You know Sheriff Brisbane?"

"No, never been there and don't know him," Daniel said.

"Judge over there name of Hatcher. He took one look at my tore up freedom papers, patched 'em back together for me and set me back to working for him."

"Working for him? I mean, for a judge?"

"To catch them runaways. He even added to the reward. Told me about a young white boy down there to Hannibal who up and ran off last night, too. Set out a reward for the white boy's safe return. Did say that if the boy was found dead, drowned or killed, he'd give up half the reward for the body."

Daniel began to sweat where he stood. The stranger talked on. "What with all the rain, Sam and me couldn't find nothing, not till we come on your light. Sam got mighty interested in your scent, too. He come braying up this way sudden as thunder. He's trained on runaways, all kinds, so I can't understand why Sam's so all-fired interested in you 'less you got a scent on you like this boy, Daniel Webster Jackson." The stranger burst out in laughter.

Daniel didn't dare move but finally asked, "What's so funny? You ain't caught nobody name of Daniel Webster Jackson."

The man kept laughing.

"My name's Effram, Effram Meriweather, and I come from St. Louis, where my pap is a blacksmith and ma's a seamstress, and they sent me on the road to see to my sick aunt in Hadleyberg. Making my way to see her now. My pap is himself down with the sickness and ma's nursing him, fearing he's going to die, and 'cept for my aunt, I ain't got no other family." Daniel began a soft crying, peeking between fingers at the man's reaction.

The man stood up and approached, coming into the light. He was a black man. Daniel stared and shook his head. "You're a slave hunter? A black man, a slave hunter?"

"Sam and me been doing it for years. We's the best."

"Slave hunting is dirty business." Daniel said boldly.

The stranger came at Daniel, his white eyes filling with the light from the entrance to the cave, his shoulders heaving forward, and his nostrils flaring like an angered bull. The dog barked at Daniel's back.

"Maybe it is, and maybe it ain't," he declared, standing right over Daniel now. "When Sam and me catches 'em, it ain't. Sam don't tear no man apart. I don't put a scratch on a man I catch. I'm proud to know a man brave 'nough to run from his master!"

The man turned from Daniel and walked toward the back of the cave again, but he stayed in the light, talking. "Slave be safer with me. Some slave runners do awful things to a man. They treats him like an animal, sometimes maim him! Some even makes their money by running the slave, and once caught, selling him or her to the market block in St. Louis for Deep South plantation work—just as if the runaway was theirs to sell! It all depends on if the reward is higher than the market prices."

"Whew!" whistled Daniel, "I aint't never heard about nobody that dishonest before."

The stranger laughed.

"You sure laugh a lot for a runaway catcher," Daniel said.

"Oh, I was laughin' before 'cause of that name, Daniel Webster Jackson! Sounds so dandified, you know, and now I'm laughing at how foolish you sound. There's plenty who'd paint you black and sell you in St. Louis, boy!"

"What's so bad about Daniel Webster Jackson? Sounds like a fine name to me, respectable!"

He just laughed more. "I'm glad it's your name and not mine," he finally said.

"But it ain't my name," Daniel protested. "My name's Effram, just like I told you, Effram Meriweather, and I come from St. Louis."

The stranger lifted the long gun which had lain so neatly along his long leg that Daniel hadn't notice it until now. He pointed it directly between Daniel's eyes. "Let's don't have no more tales, all right, Daniel?"

"If you want me to be this here Daniel Webster fellow, I guess I can be," said Daniel, raising his hands as if under arrest. "You want me to put my hands behind my back?"

"No, not at all," said the runaway catcher. "I want you to help me find them runaways. When we do, maybe you can be on your way. Judge Hatcher's got some idea you know where they may be. I want you to take me to this here Colonel Halverston's place. You're going to work the inside while I work the outside."

Daniel didn't answer. The stranger smiled. "I want to know particular about this fellow over there they calls Billy, Old Billy. How old you think he is?"

Daniel didn't answer quickly enough to suit the man who raised his gun again and said, "Like I told you, boy, I can get half reward on your dead carcass."

The bounty hunter came nearer, sizing up the silent boy. "Good, Daniel, now we can work together like old friends, can't we? It'll be just like the judge planned all along. He's going to be so happy."

Daniel frowned as the bounty hunter's smile grew wider.

CHAPTER FIVE

DOORWAY TO THE UNDERGROUND RAILROAD

The slave catcher laughed as he hurried Sam and Daniel from the cave and down the hill. He seemed in an awful hurry, and he could hardly walk straight for laughing. Over and over, he repeated Daniel's full name and asked, "Where'd you come by such a name?"

While Daniel didn't care to have his name laughed at, he knew he could do nothing about it, not just now. The slave runner kept Daniel well ahead of him in easy sight, and the dog bounded well ahead of them both. As they followed the course of the river, Daniel watched the water sparkle and reflect the morning sun. A passing keelboat looked painted on the water. Purple patches of shadow remained in the woods. A breeze played through the leaves.

On the opposite shore, Daniel saw a large, white house out on a ledge nestled among the trees. Someone placed a light in the window there every night. White folks said the light, acting as a beacon, helped guide steamers and other river traffic at night. Black folks believed it was there to guide runaway slaves over to the Illinois side during fog and storm. Old Billy said a fugitive slave would be welcomed there if he could scale the rugged cliff, and from there the runaway would be rushed to a safer place. Old Billy said that the runaway who made it up the cliff, soon found himself passed from hand to hand as human cargo on the Underground Railroad—passed along by the abolitionists clear to Canada, a country where slavery was forbidden by law.

Unsure if the story about the house on the hill was true or one of Billy's tall tales, Daniel had also heard that whenever any black person looked at the house, his look became a peculiar stare. And now, when Daniel realized that the black runaway catcher had fallen behind, he turned to find the man staring strangely up at the old house.

The man, realizing that Daniel stood staring at him, yelled to Daniel, and pointed to the house saying, "Right smart-looking place to build a home."

"They call it the door to the Underground Railroad," Daniel fired back, hoping to catch the man's reaction. *This stranger seems to know these parts better than he lets on,* Daniel thought.

"Who calls it that? Your friend, Old Billy?"

"Some black folks I heard talking once is all, Mr. Runaway Catcher."

"My name's Penny, son, Mr. George Penny."

"Okay, Mr. Penny."

"Just the same, you call me George so's to arouse no suspicions, and I'll call you Effram when we're around others." He had caught up to Daniel and shook on it. "Come on. Let's get down off this hill."

Finding level ground and open sky, they heard the first cry of black birds cawing and chasing after one another. George's keen eyes followed the clamoring birds in flight. He shaded his eyes with a large forearm. In the daylight, Daniel guessed him to be perhaps twenty-five years old.

George watched the birds until they floated earthward and dropped from sight. *He has Indian ways,* Daniel thought—w*atching fool birds fly around.*

"Settled aways off yonder," he said, pointing his long gun. "How'd you like some good eatin' breakfast, Daniel?"

Daniel gulped hard. "Ain't never tasted crow meat before; ain't sure I'd fancy it."

George broke into an uproar of laughter. "You don't eat the crows, son, you eat the corn they lead you to."

Daniel's stomach answered with a hollow growl.

Halfway across a clearing, they found the stand of dry, aged corn stalks that invited them in to pick their fill. As they watched, the dog inch forward. Daniel felt as if they were the only three living creatures on earth, save the twittering bugs. Daniel heard the early wind rustle the dried corn stalks when suddenly Sam frightened the black birds at their breakfast. Some twenty lifted with an awful caw and were gone in an instant. The noise scared George into raising his gun to fire. When he realized it was only the crows he, for once, laughed at himself.

"Corn'll be old and dry this time of year, but they always leave some good ones behind, Daniel," George said, lifting the slim leaves, knocking over weak stalks and yanking at a fat ear here and there. "We can roast these over a fire. Soften 'em up."

In little time, George had roasted several ears of corn. He sliced off kernels from the cob for Sam to eat, but the hound didn't seem to care for corn too much. "Well then, go get us a rabbit!" George told his dog.

"This is good," said Daniel, chewing on his blackened corn, the juices spilling over his lips.

"I cook it right," replied George. "It's got to be good."

They fell silent for a time, just listening to the woods. "You got some worry on your mind, don't you, Daniel?"

"Oh, no! Ain't nothing to worry me, Mr. Penny."

"You must be awful worried about something to run away from the judge just when he give you that fine job of spying. He sent me after you...to see you do your duty, son, to make him proud! And if'n I can help, I'm sure going to, but I can't help if you don't trust me. Now, what's troubling you?"

"I don't think there's anything unusual going on out to Colonel Halverston's place. Nothing Billy or the colonel'd do would go against the law! And I ain't never seen the ground open up to take anybody inside it, like they say."

"Well I did," George said, surprising Daniel. "First night Sam and me met you, but I'm new to these parts, and the posse come after me, so I run off in the wrong direction and found you, remember?"

"That was you holding that knife to my throat?"

"Me and Sam, yeah."

"Well, I only heard about the ground opening up and swallowing runaways."

"And I seen it once, near Halverston's. Who told you about it, Daniel?"

"Old Billy, but it was just one of his stories."

"I know you like Old Billy, Daniel. He tells you young'uns stories and whittles you boats and pretend swords out of piney wood, but if he and the colonel are stealing slaves, then he's breaking the law of the Missouri Compromise."

"Billy wouldn't have no truck with breaking the law."

"But if he is an outlaw, son, and you're helping keep his secrets...."

"I tell you he ain't outside the law."

"Just the other night, I was hot on finding the Coleson County runaways—Sam and me—when zingo! They disappeared right in front of us. All mighty peculiar."

Daniel felt George's eyes on him, but he didn't reply.

"That's when the posse come, and all they had left to run was me and Sam. The rest you know."

Daniel's mind returned to that night at the slave quarters. *Could Billy be guilty of slave snatching? The colonel? Would a fine-dresssing, upstanding man like him do that to make the judge look bad?* Daniel felt unsure, and he wasn't sure he liked seeing runaway slaves caught by a man like George Penny, for a bounty, to be returned to men who mistreated their slaves as the colonel had said. He wasn't even sure if there ought to be slaves—*there just always was!* Daniel often wondered why black men born just across the river in Illinois were free, while men born in Missouri were not. No one, not even Judge Hatcher, knew the answer to that one.

George reached out and shook Daniel from his thoughts, scaring him, saying, "Daniel! You want them slaves caught and sold South by someone who don't even own them? Someone who won't return them to Mr. Grimes, their righful owner?"

"No."

"Then help me. I can't find that exact spot again. I stumbled on it in the first place. So take me to see this here Billy."

"No."

"You ever hear about how it is in the Deep South for a slave, Daniel?"

Daniel stared at George's angry eyes. The usual smile and laughter in his face had been replaced by set teeth and a serious glare. Daniel's stomach felt heavy now with the roast corn.

Daniel timidly said, "Folks have told me it's warmer in the South, and there's lots of cool night breezes and fruit trees and lots to recommend the place."

"Lots of death, lots of filth," said George, "in the sugarcane fields."

"I read somewhere's that the trees are green all year almost, and the flowers grow on trees like the stars in the sky. Flowers are all over, and the sky is lower to the ground and bluer everywhere you look. Big weeping willow trees. There's lots of clear water lakes and streams filled with ducks and all kind of birds and—"

George held up a hand, interrupting, saying, "Sure 'nough, and all the houses are big mansions, all white as heaven, as close to heaven-looking as anything in this world, except for the slave houses, of course."

"But they said in that book I read that their slave houses in Deep South beats our Missouri ones," said Daniel. "They's all painted up better, you know, whitewashed!"

George broke into a laugh again. Daniel had never seen a man before who could laugh and get so serious all so quickly, except maybe Old Billy whenever he was telling a story.

Daniel defended himself, saying, "Well, it must be so! I read it in that book! I hear tell it don't even storm down there either, never even a hint of a storm."

George grimly asked, "You ever see any black men, any black women or children on their way downriver?" His voice came now like the sudden anger and growl his dog had shown in the cave.

"Sure, I seen some in St. Louis," Daniel smugly replied.

"They stop over at Hannibal sometimes, too," said George. "I saw a man there just a day ago. He was being sold South for the second time. Name was Samson, and you ain't never seen a bigger, stronger man in your life. Bigger than me he was."

"Bigger than you?"

"But he cried like a babe when I spoke to him. He looked so sad I thought he was going to make a wild break for it right there on the dock in broad daylight!"

"Really?"

"He'd have been killed by some white man if he'd tried to jump from that slave boat. He truly didn't want no truck with the Deep South. He didn't want to see the heaven your books talk about, Daniel, 'cause he'd already seen it.

He told me he'd rather I shot him down dead where he stood."

Daniel shook his head in disbelief. "How do I know you ain't just making all this up?"

"Daniel, Samson had been sold downriver first time when he was a boy your age. Then he got traded upriver, and now he's traded back again. He felt sore afraid to be going back—said he thought he had become a free man when he hit Missouri. Said he found life here so easy, though he still be some man's slave."

Daniel began thinking of the sight of nine black people, chained one to another, asleep between bails of cotton on a flatboat he'd watched inch into the landing at Hannibal one day. Daniel thought it ironic that the first free black man he had ever met turned out to be so low-down, mean and thoughtless to his own kind as George Penny must be, a man catching runaways for reward money. *Nothing but a bounty hunter is what George amounted to,* Daniel told himself. *Yet, he talks so kindly toward Sampson and the other people he hunted. Why?* Daniel wondered.

"I know the law says that running down runaway slaves is all right, but don't you find it hard? I mean, don't it bother you any?" Daniel asked.

"Bothers you white folk more than me," Penny answered, his sly smile returning.

Daniel again shook his head, wondering if this man cared about anyone or anything. Then George began talking as if to himself. "When John Law says a man is a legal slave, there ain't no use in his running away, Daniel. Just causes more problems for everybody concerned, and it's money in the bank for me. Even if a slave gets caught way up to Ohio, Michigan, or Minnesota, he's fair game for the likes of me. I catches him and brings him back."

"You can bring 'em back from them faraway places?"

"That's what the Missouri Compromise law is all about. A fugitive slave ain't safe from capture and return from anywhere in any of these so-called free states, and who am I to question the law, let alone break it? May's well help it and help myself, I say."

Daniel had heard of the law, and he knew runaway slaves knew about it, too. This was why the aim of every runaway slave was to make it to Canada. But many did stop in friendly Quaker towns or in settlements of free Northern black people and friendly abolitionist ministers. There they'd be caught, sometimes after ten years or more, and returned South. Daniel had heard stories about runaways who'd started new lives in the North, raised families, and then were captured and returned to slavery.

"I just don't see how a black man can hunt down other black men!" Daniel finally shouted.

"White men hunt other white men who break the law," George snapped back. "Besides, I'm not just a black man. I'm a free black man—protected by freeman's own laws—the white man's laws, which tell me I can earn a trade at hunting runaways the same as any white man! I got freedom papers signed by the Governor of Illinois. I got myself free, and I got papers."

"You got free? How'd you do it? Did your master turn you free? Did you buy up yourself with wages, or did you run away yourself?"

"Everybody's running away from something," the catcher smiled in answer.

"You sure laugh a lot for a man in such a serious business."

"Guess I do."

"Well, did you or didn't you?"

"Did I what?"

"Run away yourself?"

He leaned in toward Daniel. "See this?" he said, pushing back his shirt collar to reveal an awful scar. He pulled up his shirt sleeves, revealing old scars circling his wrists. He didn't have to say any more. He'd been a slave at one time or another.

"How then can you run others who escape?" Daniel pleaded. "How do you sleep nights with yourself?"

"I don't. I sleep with Samuel!" he said with the smile Daniel had tired of. "Look here, your judge and your sheriff down at Hannibal know they can catch more rabbits if they get a fox who looks like a rabbit in among the rabbits!" He slapped his knee and laughed again. "And so long as there's slavery, there'll be rabbits running and men like your sheriff who'll chase 'em. At least I'm not going to shoot no rabbits, gut them, hang them or cut off their feet."

Frowning, Daniel recalled seeing handbills people left on the landing down at the Hannibal pier—handbills offering money for runaway slaves. One offered a hundred dollars for a slave named May. She could be returned to a Mr. Flotsam, ten miles west of Hattiesburg, Mississippi.

The bill described the girl as seventeen, eighteen or possibly twenty years old. She stood five foot four. She had all except four of her teeth, was light complexioned with a sharp nose, looked Cajun, could pass for white and liked to disguise herself as white. But she was given to the fits, and when in a fit, she'd curse and bite herself uncontrollably. The bill said she was comely for a black girl, and uncommon smart.

"You want me to go down to Hannibal and pick up some wanted posters on any runaways that I *can* find?" Daniel meanly asked.

"You just do like you're told, and we'll get on, you and me. I'll let you go off any ways you want—back to the judge or the territory West, whatever suits you—once you take me back to where the colonel's house stands. Once I've had a chance to talk to this old man Billy, you can go free."

"I'll hold you to that."

"All you gots to do is show me the countryside hereabouts. That don't make you a spy, if'n you don't want to be one, and it don't mean you are catching any runaways, if'n you don't like it. But try to trick me—just once—and I'll drown you in the river and return your carcass for the bounty the judge put out on you."

"What guarantee I got you won't go back on your word and take me back to Hannibal anyway?"

"None of us got any guarantees in this life, Daniel." George stood up and kicked dirt over the campfire, lifting his long gun as he did so. "Looks good for a black man to be traveling with a white boy. Like as if I was carrying your gun for you, young Massa' Daniel. I mean, Effram. If anyone spots us, that's how we're going to play it, you understand, Effram?"

"Why?"

"Saves time in jailhouses and time talking."

"All right," Daniel agreed, getting up.

"Now, take me to see your friend Billy."

CHAPTER SIX

THE INSIDE OF THE WORLD

As Daniel and George Penny approached Colonel Halverston's plantation by day, Daniel realized just how old the structure was. Fences needed mending. Outhouses, the livery and the tack house, along with the smoke house were all crumbling. Even the great house stood in disrepair, although at one time it must have looked grand with its four stories, its large columns, bay windows, wraparound porch, and balcony. There was nothing else like it in all of Hannibal County. At one time it must surely have looked as fine as anything in the Deep South. Still, nowadays, Daniel knew it showed a good deal better in the soft, green darkness of an evening. In daylight, the big house needed paint in the worst way, the porch and balcony needed mending, and the windows could use a good washing. Each large white pillar showed cracks and wear. The rooftop, visible from this distance, looked in need of repair work, too. Weeds and wildflower bushes threatened to eat the place whole.

"Some mansion," muttered George, unimpressed.

"It's old," apologized Daniel.

"How old is old?"

"Don't know. Maybe fifty years."

"Oh, really? That old, huh?" George fought down another laugh.

"But Colonel Halverston's only been owning it for maybe seven years."

"Then nobody around these parts knows much about this here colonel of yours, huh?"

"Not hardly much, no. He stays pretty much to himself. Lives here with his wife—Miss Amanda—Billy calls her, and they farm enough to get by."

"Aside from Old Billy, how many slaves does the man work?"

"They ain't like most slaves I know."

"How many?"

"They smile a lot, and they like the colonel and Miss Amanda."

"How many?"

"Nine, maybe ten, counting Old Billy."

George snickered and shook his head, saying, "Is that all? Ain't hardly enough to call a plantation." George then crouched in the brush and pointed to the slave quarters, a row of log houses. "Quarters look better than any I ever seen."

"Fresh paint," commented Daniel, kneeling beside the catcher.

"Each with its own chimney for cooking and warmth in winter. These slaves got it easy. Looks like your colonel spends his money on something other than his horses and Miss Amanda's evening gowns."

"He's running for judge of these here parts."

"Judge? But you all have a judge already."

"Judge Hatcher's worried the colonel might win the next election."

"Aha! So...that's why he's got me bobcatting out here. Suspects the colonel's hiding something. Why else a man would want the judge's job? And I'm not surprised by the look of this place how your colonel come under suspicion."

"Whataya mean?'

"He ain't no plantation man, just getting by on crops." George set to thinking, squinting up at the colonel's house. "Just what's this colonel a colonel of?"

Daniel blew out air, exasperated with all the questions. He then told George what he had overheard at the courthouse about how Halverston had resigned his commission at West Point and about the colonel's involvement in the Mexican War.

"Mysterious man, this colonel." George rubbed his chin. "Maybe he might win the election on being mysterious. The way Missouri elects officials, I wouldn't wonder. Might explain how your Judge Hatcher ever got elected."

While George laughed at his own joke, Daniel defended the judge, saying, "Judge Hatcher's a nice man."

"Maybe he is, maybe he ain't, but either way, he's a little dumb, but he did save me from one mean lawman."

"Sheriff Brisbane?"

"He was going to beat me again while two others held me down, and if I didn't talk, he threatened to sell me to slavers."

"Sell you?"

"And he was talking Deep South. He made that plain clear enough."

Daniel waved this off, saying, "Sheriff Brisbane's always full of threats."

"Sounded as if he meant to run me to St. Louis himself, put me on the auction block there. Said he knew a dealer there could get five hundred for a healthy, young black buck like me."

"Sheriff said that, just like that? You being truthful with me?"

"Truthful as that tree yonder," he replied, pointing to the exact tree where Old Billy and Colonel Halverston had hidden two of the Coleson County runaways. George stood now and marched directly for the slave quarters, saying, "Let's meet your friend the storyteller, now!"

Daniel tried to keep pace while Sam, the dog, leapt ahead of them. "What'd you say to Sheriff Brisbane to change his mind?"

"Didn't change his mind. Changed the judge's mind when I showed him my foot."

"Your foot?"

"Took off my boot and showed the two of them my clubfoot."

"What clubfoot?" Daniel hadn't seen the man so much as favor either foot or limp once.

"Told them that even with my special-made boot, I couldn't work no sugarcane field for no more'n an hour at a time. Foot gets so bad, I can't bear it. Told 'em I wasn't worth not even fifty dollars, let alone five hundred. Told 'em my boots cost more than I was worth. Judge Hatcher told me to quit talking money and start talking smarts."

"Is that all true."

"Every word."

"I mean about your foot."

"Showed 'em my foot, yeah."

"But we've been walking all morning long."

George shrugged. "The boot works wonders, and I have my good days."

"I'd have never known. I still don't know which foot it is," said Daniel, staring at George's feet.

"And you won't ever know. I take the pain like a man."

Someone yelled from behind them, shouting, "Daniel? Who you got there?"

Daniel and George turned to see several children surrounding the legs of a white-haired black man, Old Billy, where he stood atop a rise, looking sternly down on the two intruders. "What brings you here this time-a-day?"

⧖ ⧖ ⧖

Daniel sat for over an hour outside the cabin where Old Billy and George Penny talked, unable to hear a word, with Sam resting over his feet and some of the black children playing around him. He scoured the area with his eyes, plotted out a hundred escape routes and imagined fifty attempts. Going on dusk now, he realized that George had simply taken it for granted that Sam would keep Daniel in check. Still, he thought George was uncommonly careless with his white runaway.

Inside the old cabin, Billy continued to talk, and the men often burst out in laughter. The runaway catcher couldn't possibly have told Billy his true identity, Daniel guessed. Now Daniel snatched his feet from under the snoring dog, stood and walked around in larger circles, testing just how far from the cabin and the dog he might get before someone discovered him. Not ten feet off, Sam roused himself, stretched, yawned and then glared at Daniel. Suddenly, Old Billy's cabin door opened and out stepped George, followed by Billy, who was in turn followed by two large, black men. Strangers to Daniel, these men glared meanly at him. The four grownups marched right for Daniel, and for the first time ever, Daniel felt afraid of Old Billy.

Billy rushed to step between Daniel and the others, saying, "Young Daniel, we been all talking with Mr. Penny here, the man you brought to us, and we want to ask you to please go with him and do as he says."

"Go where?"

"Will you take your orders from him, Daniel?" asked Billy. "Will you trust me? Put yourself in Mr. Penny's hands for now. It's important, Daniel."

"But...but George said I could go once we found you."

"Please, Daniel. These men here, you know they's the Coleson County runaways, and they're for —"

"I don't know that; don't want to know that."

Old Billy took him aside and whispered, "They want to kill you, boy; hide your carcass over in them woods yonder, Dan. Now do as I tells you." Billy's face showed his fright.

George joined them, saying, "Allow me a word with my young associate, gentlemen. Daniel, you didn't want to spy for the judge, not on your friend, Billy. We all have to respect you for that. I like Old Billy, and I like these boys from Coleson."

"So...so do I," managed Daniel.

"Now hear me out. These boys've given over their souls to the Devil to make free, and you led me right to 'em, son. You can understand why they're worried you might do the same for the judge! Now, here's what Old Billy and I propose. There's a man over at Rantul County, name of Blainy, and you know the way to his farmhouse. You take me there and help me get what I want, and I'll let Billy and these runaways go on about their business. I won't take you back to Hannibal, either."

Old Billy, George and the others waited for an answer. George finally said, "Rantul's a far place from here, Billy tells me."

"Why do you want to see this man, Blainy?"

"That don't concern you. He ain't no relation to you, is he?"

Daniel thought longer. Old Billy pleaded, "Do it, Daniel, please. These men'll be sold to Deep South if'n they're caught."

"I'll do it if you show me how you did it," said Daniel. "You show me how you made them disappear way over there and come again in that tree there, and I'll do it."

All of the men conferred with some arguing. Finally, Old Billy said, "We've gotta give it up anyway. The law's getting too near. They're going to sniff it out. Come on!"

Old Billy led them to the next rise and down into a cleft valley. He directed them toward a clump of trees, standing in a foreboding dark circle. As they walked along, George stared in every direction about the ground until his dog sniffed out one spot in particular. Daniel then saw George go for a large rock and lift it. He feared they had tricked him, that George would hit him over the head with the rock any second now. Instead, George pulled a buckskin pouch from under the stone and stuffed it under his shirt.

"Something I lost here the other night," he confided in everyone, and Daniel felt relief, seeing that George had dropped the stone.

It had come on darkness when Old Billy said, "Now all of you just take off running and hollering, right toward those trees and hills yonder! Go!"

With that Daniel let go with a war-whoop and all of them ran, yelling and whooping like Indians on the warpath. When they reached the area, Daniel heard a screeching noise and saw a light coming from out of a gaping hole amid the shadows. Someone stood there, a lantern in his hand, motioning them onward and shouting, "Come on! This way, hurry!"

Daniel and George stared at one another, amazed. The two runaways had been here before, and this time they went in unafraid. George and Daniel held back until Daniel saw that the man holding the lantern proved to be Colonel Halverston himself. Halverston stared out at Old Billy, and he had a look in his eye that would melt ice.

"Who's this white boy, Billy? What's he doing here?"

"Daniel's all right, colonel. He won't make no trouble for us."

"Trouble's already come for you, colonel," George said to Halverston. "The judge and sheriff're getting too close to the operation. You have to close this station down, and fast."

"Who're you to tell me what to do?"

"Colonel—" began Billy.

"Shut up, Billy," the colonel angrily replied, then turned to George. "I asked you, mister, just who are you?"

"Name's George Penny. I'm a free black man. I was sent to snoop around these parts by Judge Hatcher, and I'm due back to report to him anytime now."

"Why're you telling me all this then?" The colonel stood tall and firm, holding his lantern to George's features, studying him.

"Colonel, we should get inside and talk," said Billy. "It won't do for someone to see us all out here."

The colonel nodded, saying, "Follow me."

The opening was only large enough for one man to enter at a time. The entrance proved pitch black, the cavern cold and silent except for the light trickle of an underground stream. It all gave Daniel the shivers, but once inside, the colonel raised the wick on his lantern and held it closer to the entrance. Daniel saw that a stone slab, perhaps five by four feet, moved by two pulleys and was worked within a guiding wood frame that hugged the cave walls. One of the colonel's house servants grinned at Daniel from where he stood at the cranking pulley.

"I learned a little engineering in my army days," said the colonel. "Come along."

In a matter of minutes, the group was passing through one of the most beautiful underground caverns Daniel had ever seen. The walls sparkled blue with silver flashes wherever the colonel's light fell. Here and there, Daniel spied a shiny wet wall of orange where clay sediment accumulated, the water trickling over it to form a stream at their feet. Big gray, saltlike rocks hung from the ceiling, each looking to Daniel like an upside down dunce cap. Wherever the colonel's light failed to penetrate, this place was in total darkness.

"No wonder there's so many tales about this place," Daniel said aloud, his words echoing through the cavern. "Looks like the inside of the world."

"Only the bravest come through when they see the earth open its mouth to take them in," replied the colonel from the front of the line. Then the colonel and Old Billy resumed whispering.

They now passed from one open area to the next, through narrow passageways, connected in places by mere holes where they crawled through on their stomachs, getting their shirts wet with red clay and wet dirt. At times, Daniel felt like a lizard as they descended into the earth. As they went deeper, it became colder, until the walls were icy. George and the house servant followed Daniel, urging him onward.

Eventually, the angle of the floor carried them upwards rather than down. They continued up for a long time, and suddenly they approached ladder rungs. They passed stone masonry walls now, and Daniel recognized the walls as the foundation and supports of oak beams, split four inches square, framing the entry into a root cellar. Daniel looked around when everyone had come through the trap door. The cellar walls shone thick with the cut of stone blocks, their surface ragged here, smooth there. The wood shelves around held flour, vegetables, jars, preserves, wines, and meals. Corn tied in large bundles dangled neatly from the ceiling. Flour sacks sat alongside bushel baskets full with tomatoes, potatoes, squash, onions and beets. Another set of stairs was illuminated from the light of the house, where a door stood open to another trap door. Daniel now realized the root cellar sat below the house, not outside or back of the house.

At the second trap door, a face appeared and a woman shouted down, "Is all well, dear?"

She was the colonel's wife. The colonel looked up and answered, "Don't worry, Amanda. It was just a drill. The cargo has arrived a second time. They just had a round-trip ticket and wanted to cash it in."

Daniel wondered what the colonel meant by calling them all cargo, and what he meant by "ticket" and "cashing in." George had called this place a station. Then he realized since this was part of the underground railroad, of course they called it a station, and the cargo was the Coleson County men, and they had a ticket to ride on the train.

"Come," said Colonel Halverston, taking a bottle from one of the slots on the wine rack. "We'll talk upstairs in comfort, Mr. Penny."

CHAPTER SEVEN

DANIEL'S ESCAPE

"How'd you get started doing the work of the Underground Railroad? Who do you pass your cargo on to, once the cargo leaves your hands?" asked George, holding his wine glass as if he didn't know what to do with it. They sat in the colonel's beautiful den, the walls lined with what Daniel believed must be every book ever written. "I mean, I thought I knew all about the road along the Mississppi, every station. But I never heard tell of you before, and you do it so neatly, I know there's got to be talk."

The colonel replied, "Talk is what kills people, you know. A slip of the lip, all that."

"But not if you turn the talk into just that—talk—the ghost story, the fanciful tale of some poor idiot storyteller," added Mrs. Halverston.

"Like Old Billy?" asked George.

Old Billy wasn't there to hear himself called names. He'd taken the runaways to a safer place, Daniel guessed. "Mr. Billy ain't no idiot," Daniel protested. "He's smart, really, he is."

The colonel lifted his glass and toasted Daniel's statement, saying, "That he is and a fine man! He could go North, make free anytime on my line," boasted the colonel.

"But he'd rather stay and help the others out. He has people who are loyal to him," Mrs. Halverston added.

"We don't take on a new person unless we're certain of him," said Halverston, sipping at his wine. "Even some black men have an attitude, drilled into them by society, that running away is not only illegal, that it's immoral, religiously wrong."

"They get it with their food, their wash, their board and their preachers," said Mrs. Halverston.

"We can't be too careful here," added the colonel.

"You're not being careful at all, colonel, taking to this man!" Daniel bravely stepped forward and declared. "He's a runaway catcher himself, a bounty hunter!"

"That may be, Daniel," replied Halverston, "but he seems a man of his word, and from what Billy tells me, I think we can trust him to keep our secret. He's made a deal with Old Billy—your help for the runaways."

"But I ain't worth nothing, and when he finds out, he'll be coming right back here with Sheriff Brisbane and Judge Hatcher."

The colonel and George looked at one another and smiled. The colonel, chuckling, said, "You go on out to the kitchen to find something to eat, son. You must be hungry."

"Yes, go ahead, Daniel. We'll just chat a while longer," said George.

Daniel's frown and raised shoulders displayed his exasperation, but he only walked off. He closed the door as the colonel answered another of George's questions, saying, "I quit when the military completely let me down. I had been a military lawyer, and was given a case to defend having to do with a young private charged with cowardice and hung as an example when his entire platoon had run from the scene of a battle."

Mrs. Halverston said, "The young man was chosen and condemned on one fact alone. He was a Negro. He wasn't even carrying a gun into battle. He was hardly more than Daniel's age. He was the bugler and carried the flag."

"And they convicted him over my objections and any reason, and all I could do was watch them murder him in the grandest of military fashion," said Halverston, swallowing hard, as if it had happened only yesterday.

Old Billy stood in the hall as Daniel closed the door. "The colonel don't want to give up the station, not for a day, that's plain. If he could win that election, we could go into a whole new operation. He's worried plenty he won't win. Lots on his mind," Billy finished.

One of the Coleson runaways stood beside Billy. "He's the finest White man I ever did meet," he said to Billy.

Daniel felt mighty confused, wishing to ask a hundred questions. He began by asking, "How? How do you do it? I know the colonel came up from the cave right as we ran into those trees shouting, but I don't figure he's guarding the entrance twenty-four hours a day."

"We have our signals, Daniel," Old Billy said, smiling. "They were all around you, all day long."

Daniel thought and thought. "I saw no signals sent from you to the colonel's house."

Old Billy shrugged. "Not the sheriff, not no one ever sees what they're looking right at. And the most overlooked and underestimated people in the world are little ones, tiny ones just out of diapers. We send 'em back and forth to the quarters and the colonel's house."

"How can you trust babes with getting the message right?"

"Don't trust 'em with the message. They are the message! All they know is they're going up to the big house to beg scraps, or take a pail of peas or a snatch of carrots to the cook. Any other time, the cook gets her own fixings."

Daniel mulled this over. He shook his head, nodding in understanding. "Can you tell me why that bounty hunter is all of a sudden no longer interested in the Coleson runaways, and now wants to take out to Rantul County after Mr. Blainy? He ain't looking to kill Mr. Blainy, is he?"

Old Billy laughed. "What an imagination this boy's got! Kill a white man? Even a free black man knows better'n that!"

"What's he going there for then?"

Old Billy dropped his gaze. "I can't tell you that, Daniel. You'll have to ask him yourself. He's got his reasons."

Daniel stared at the white-haired old man, saying nothing.

Billy added, "Look here, you don't have to care about his reasons. All you have to do is get him there. Besides, with Judge Hatcher and the sheriff on the lookout for you,

you'll be safer in Rantul territory for awhile. Then you can come on back."

"Don't figure to ever come back."

"Sure you can."

"Judge'll want to know why I ran."

"Tell him you come out here to do your spying job, and you got lost is all, and a kindly family took you in, taking pity on you, and you stayed with them until they brought you back to Hannibal."

"I don't know as I want to come back, Billy."

"You ain't got no other place, Daniel. You got to come back."

Daniel didn't answer. He sat thinking.

"Look here," began Billy, "you can say you was snatched and kidnapped. I'll write out a ransom note. No, we'll have the colonel do the job. He can write a real smart letter. You can say you escaped after we send the letter down to the judge. It'll be a real adventure to be kidnapped, ransomed and escaped, Daniel."

"That's a real smart idea," agreed Daniel with a smile. "But you don't understand. I ain't wanting to go back to living under Mrs. Shorr's care, nor always running to the judge whenever I got a problem, nor being sent to him for a lecture each time I gall Mrs. Shorr or someone else around Hannibal. I think I want to take out on my own, take up manly work, maybe light out for the Territory."

"Well, you just get that notion right outta your head, boy. Maybe that'd be all right for some, but you ain't near ready yet, Daniel." Old Billy's tone meant he did not want to say another word on the subject.

Daniel's arms dropped to his sides. He started for the kitchen area at the back of the big house. "Guess I'll go find something to eat."

"You go right on, son."

On the way to the kitchen, Daniel had to pass the small alcove from which the trapdoor led down into the root cellar. He glanced at the rug thrown over the trapdoor. He stole a look back to where Old Billy stood. It bothered Daniel that Old Billy and Colonel Halverston were being hornswoggled by the runaway catcher, and that Billy seemed not to trust Daniel with any information regarding George's plans for this man Blainy. He also wondered what might be in George's buckskin pouch now on the leather strap around his neck. *What's so important that he'd hide it from the others, keeping it close to his chest?*

The mystery of the opening earth and the appearance of Satan carrying a lantern and beckoning the slaves into the bowels of the blackest hole in creation had been solved, at least for Daniel. He felt frustrated now with an even more mysterious question, a strange, black freeman who was supposed to be catching runaway slaves, but who instead made bargains and let the slaves go free. What was the runaway catcher's game? Who was Blainy to him? And why did Daniel Webster Jackson have to get bargained off by his friend, Old Billy, when it was for Old Billy's sake that he'd run away from home in the first place? Nothing seemed fair, and everything was confusing; the trapdoor appeared the only way out for him.

Daniel jumped at the chance, stepping quickly into the hidden alcove. Not hearing any objections, he lifted the rug and pulled up the latch. The door creaked ever so quietly, but not lightly enough to suit him. He finally raised it all the way and realized how dark the interior was, but in the square of light spilling into the cellar he saw the colonel's lamp alongside some stick matches. He lowered the door over his head and went for the lantern in the dark, knocking over some jars on the table. He lit the light without any further difficulty, studying the room for anything he might wish to take with him. He stuffed his pocket with a potato and yanked off an ear of corn. He saw some jars and examined them more closely. He found some paint, lampblack and molasses. The molasses was good. It would be rich, like candy. He could survive for days on it, he told himself. In the second he decided, Daniel heard footsteps overhead. He located and emptied a gunnysack of potatoes that rolled out like rocks, and then he placed several jars, the corn and some squash inside the sack.

He rushed down the cellar stairs, lantern in hand, into the depths of the waiting cavern. In a matter of minutes, he found himself squeezing through the tunnels, holding the lantern carefully, pushing the sack ahead of him. He feared he'd find himself hopelessly lost at every turn. When he did finally arrive in the area of the entranceway, he felt certain that when he moved the stone, he'd find George, the colonel, Old Billy or Sheriff Brisbane and his posse waiting on the other side. He took some minutes of thought before moving the rock, but when he did, he found the night woods empty and silent, as quiet as a grave. He found himself alone—alone and free to run.

CHAPTER EIGHT

NIGHT OF THE SILENT DOGS

The thick, rich molasses filled Daniel somewhat after he'd roasted his ear of corn and potato and eaten them. He cursed himself for not having picked up more, because the squash proved too old for anything other than a gourd. One jar of molasses turned out to be a jar of lampblack. Still, no matter how hungry he might get from here on, he felt good; he was free.

Daniel now listened to the sounds of the river, having camped along its bank after a northerly trek. He'd thought that direction a wise decision, believing George would think him too dumb to continue on toward Rantul County. But he planned to steer clear of any farmsteads or plantations, especially those of the Blainy clan.

Alone as he now was, Daniel relaxed, staring out over the stillness of the great Mississippi River, thinking just how calm nature could be. *Generally,* he told himself, *things prove peaceful and quiet, and there isn't too much involved in simple living. You just sit or stretch out, lie your head on as soft a rock as could be found and stare up into the moonlit night sky, counting stars.*

Excitement was the exception, as when a person met somebody like George Penny, a black self-professed runaway catcher. Exception was also when a body stumbled onto the Underground Railroad. George had confided that Halverston's operation was just one of thousands of railway stations all along the river, extending as far south as Louisiana where the Mississippi spilled into the ocean, and as far north as Minnesota, where the Mississippi River originated, he said, as a trickle of water from the earth. Said it began as a trifling stream, so small you could step across it in a single step.

"That's the trouble with Mr. Penny," he told the night air. "He comes out with the most marvelous facts one moment, some useful information, and he can train you on how best to catch a squirrel or decide how prosperous a man is by sizing things up, but then in the next breath out comes a whopper like that about the Mississippi. He even went so far as to say he'd seen it with his own eyes . How you going to trust a man who'd lie about a natural wonder like the Mississippi?"

Daniel was wondering if all free black men were as strange as Mr. Penny, when a sudden clatter of shouting and dogs braying from upriver alerted him.

Daniel leapt to his feet and kicked sand over his fire until it stopped smoldering. He searched for a decent place to hide, but nothing seemed safe. Then he recalled how the runaways had hidden that night at Halverston's, up in a tree. He looked for a sturdy tree nearby, one with a slim enough trunk to climb, or one with a low-hanging branch. He found a strong one and pulled himself off the ground. Just as he did so, several black men, one barely his own age, came barreling into his campsite, looking in all directions, shouting at one another. One stood tall and strong-looking, and he seemed the group leader. "This way," he shouted, pointing to the lower river trail. "Gots to be this way!"

"No, Eben!" shouted a second man, not quite so tall. "We're done for if'n they catch us, and they're onto our trail! I don't care what that white man friend of yours said no more."

"That white man'll be gettin' us killed, Eben!" shouted a third.

"This way!" the one called Eben repeated, still pointing in the same direction before starting ahead. Then he turned to face all the others, who now stood against him. "We got to do as planned. If we're caught, we're caught. But the finding of the main line, the line on the freedom train Sheriff Brisbane told me about, that's what we got to find, and he says it'll be a barge a-waiting for us on the river, this way!"

"How you know you can trust a white lawman?"

"Without help from the Underground Railroad, how're we going to make a thousand miles to Canada, boys?"

The leader moved off, leaving the others for only a moment before they rushed after Eben. The one who'd objected in the beginning stepped squarely onto Daniel's campfire ashes. Having no shoes on, he burned his feet and went out howling and hopping after the others.

Daniel's thoughts raced. He knew that Sheriff Brisbane had nothing to do with Colonel Halverston's station on the Underground Railroad. The sheriff must have been talking about the disappearances on Halverston's land, and these slaves must have overheard.

Then the dogs came running and snarling into camp, stopped for a few moments, sniffing all about. They were all catch dogs, trained on runaways. A catch dog was of bloodhound stock, not like George's black-and-tan, Samuel. These dogs ranged in color from yellow to sand brown. Bred from birth for chasing men, they stayed low to the ground, running close in a pack like wolves, yelping, falling over one another, and at times jumping clean over one another like children at leapfrog in their pursuit. They were clean dogs, kept lean and snarly. Their ribs showed on each side below their haunches. They had short fur, and long snouts for scenting. Sleek runners, they were faster than any man.

The dogs disappeared after the runaways as fast as they'd come. Fortunately, they paid no heed to any other scent. As soon as the dogs ran off, the men chasing after them came into the clearing. Seeing that this posse was led by Sheriff Brisbane and the fellow called Lem, Daniel felt his heart in his throat. He tightened his grip on the limb and prayed no one in the posse wanted to count stars tonight.

"Listen," said Lem to the others, raising a hand. Several of them seemed about to drop, and they leaned against trees and rocks, huffing. The runaways had given them a hard time. "Listen," repeated Lem, "do you all hear that?"

"Hear what?"

"I don't hear nothing."

Hardly able to breathe, Sheriff Brisbane said, "What're you yammering about, Lem?" The sheriff stood near Daniel's campfire which having just been stirred, sent an ember or two skyward. Daniel watched Brisbane inch closer and closer to his fire; he'd be discovered in a matter of minutes, he feared.

Instead, the sheriff turned on Lem and said, "None of us hears anything." He saw that all the others were now intently listening for the dogs.

Daniel realized that the dogs had gone silent, as though they'd fallen asleep! Just minutes before, they had torn after the runaways, braying to the moon. He'd heard their barking and yelping as it faded in the distance, but now there was nothing.

"Oh, yeah," said the sheriff, realizing, "the dogs!"

"Strange, ain't it?" asked Lem.

"Unnatural is what it is," replied Brisbane. "Like as if they fell off a cliff, or into some hole and were killed or something."

"Like the night you lost your dog, sheriff," said Lem. "But that was way down to Hannibal, near Halverston's."

"I know that," snarled Sheriff Brisbane.

They fell silent, listening. "I don't like it none," Lem finally said.

"Stop this foolishness. Next thing you'll be telling me the Devil opened up the earth and swallowed 'em all whole, like that fool Old Billy tells it. You going to believe that, Lem?"

"Truthful, sheriff, I don't know no more what to believe. Reverend Thornbush told his congregation that it's possible Old Billy could be right."

"Reverend Thornbush said that, did he?" Sheriff Brisbane shook his head. "Well if the Reverend's willing to believe it..."

"Said the Lord works in mysterious ways."

"Said that, he did?" asked Brisbane, rubbing his chin.

"Says that God allows his way with sinners, and he says there's no worse sinner than a runaway slave, 'cause that slave is stealing himself from his master, that it's same as taking another man's horse or cow."

"'Course it's stealing," replied the sheriff. "Every time a slave runs off, it lowers the price you may get for him, unless you're smart enough to keep it to yourself." He chuckled at this, and some of the men joined him.

All was quiet again before Lem asked, "Which way you 'spose they went, sheriff?"

Sheriff Brisbane—bragged about as the best tracker in all of Hannibal County—turned his face west and pointed in the opposite direction of the fleeing slaves. Daniel watched, amazed. Then the sheriff eased out at a trot, his heavy bulk bouncing as he said, "If the Devil is giving these runaways what's due 'em, then I'm absolute certain whether we catch them or not, they will pay dearly for their fool, sinful ways. If not in this life, then in the next, which is a sight worse."

Lem and the others blindly followed the sheriff westward without benefit of the dogs to tell them they were on the wrong path.

Daniel didn't shinny down from the tree for some time. He held on, thinking either the sheriff had been completely fooled by Billy's old tale, or that he was lying to the others. *Maybe he's become so tired, he wants to give up the chase and leave the runaways in God's and Satan's hands. That would explain why he hadn't taken his men on down the river trail, knowing as he must that the slaves footprints pointed in that direction. Of course, the sheriff might be so afraid of being snatched by Satan himself that he feared following the slaves! Still, why the sudden silence of the dogs?*

Lem was right; they were too far from Colonel Halverston's for Old Billy and the colonel to have had anything to do with the disappearance of these slaves or the dogs. Could there be another cavern, another Underground Railway station nearby here? Mr. Penny said there are thousands of stations and hundreds of lines, each specializing in its own brand of cargo. He said there are as many kinds of station houses as men who ran them: barns, silos, caves, houses, churches, cellars, attics, stagecoach line shacks, and even barges and boats! He also said that every man who helps a slave to freedom has his own reasons for doing so. Just as there are many who do it on principle and feeling—there are as many who do it for money. The slave often has to pay his transporter when he first gets on the railroad.

Then a thought bit Daniel like a rattler, surprising him, making him wonder that he could have such a thought. *Could Sheriff Brisbane himself be an Underground Railroad agent? The dogs are his; the territory is his; even the posse is his. What a disguise for an abolitionist, if he is one. It must be a slave's dream come true to have the help of a white sheriff.* He recalling the runaway, Eben, who so thoroughly trusted the sheriff.

Daniel wondered if Lem or any of the others were in cahoots with the sheriff. He wondered if the sheriff's station might be a house down the road, a barn, or a mill. But he didn't recall having seen one. *A cave,* he thought. *It must be a cave along the river, and there'd be someone waiting who knew the dogs well and would lather them down, feeding and watering them. No wonder the dogs fell silent.*

The station could as well be a boat, a barge, maybe a large flatboat, he thought, recalling the big one he'd seen out in the storm the night he ran away from Hannibal. He wondered now if that might be the sheriff's own freedom-boat, setting out into the storm to carry cargo across to the Illinois side of the river. Suddenly, Sheriff Brisbane became for Daniel the most brave, courageous man he'd ever known, besides Old Billy and Colonel Halverston. Getting caught, or having to go back to Hannibal, didn't seem so frightening anymore.

Finally, Daniel climbed down from the tree and searched for the gunnysack of supplies he'd tossed behind a boulder. He decided to locate a safer place to camp for the night. He wore a smile on his face; he felt better about Hannibal people, about Missouri people, about white people, about all people.

CHAPTER NINE

LIES IN DISGUISE

Daniel scanned the lay of the land, the houses, barn, tannery, smoke house, and slave quarters. Every now and again, he saw movement, men putting up horses for the night, pitching hay, driving cows to stalls, or locking chicken roosts against foxes and hungry travelers like himself. Daniel had seen the place off in the distance, and he'd thought to enter by night to steal some eggs. An egg would taste so much better right now than another fingertip of molasses. He'd had his fill of the sticky, gummy syrup.

He had seen the first farmhouse light come on from a half mile off. Any light showing through the bleak forest at night felt friendly and inviting, warm and human. Daniel crouched, coming in carefully now, just as he'd seen the runaway catcher do. He lay belly down in the tall grass on the outskirts of the old place, sizing up the farmstead. He watched the hands, several busy black men. One looked to be a mechanic who had learned how to fix a pump. He saw others at work near the barn. He tripled the figure of slaves he saw on the property to get a fair estimate of how many people the place supported. Two other black men worked to unhitch some mules and bed them down. A small carriage with a frilly fringe all around its top sat out front with yet another black man holding the reins. He smoked a cigar and wore a fine red suit, and he seemed to be putting on airs, too proud to talk to the other black people.

It had been two days since Daniel had seen another human being, and here everyone appeared to be turning in for the night. His hunger pains told him to turn back to Hannibal, give himself up, that he wasn't cut out for the pioneer life. But, just then the side door entrance to the big house opened on a screeching pair of rusty hinges, and onto the little side porch stepped the largest woman Daniel had ever seen. The weight of her made the porch boards sag and groan, as did the steps as she took each. She turned toward the henhouse, perhaps going for some eggs herself. Daniel counted her steps as she went, figuring how many steps it would take him to get from his grass cover to the henhouse himself.

The woman shouted for the man at the henhouse to open it up for her. Daniel thought, *She must be an important house servant, used to giving orders.* Her owl-eyed stare cut distance in half, and for a moment, Daniel imagined she could see him where he lay. In fact, her eyes lit on him and stayed there for some time, as if she could feel him there. Daniel tried to shake the feeling.

She abruptly lifted her stare and began humming an old spiritual song, sad with low dips and moaning. Daniel thought it sounded a bit like crying. Still, as she returned from the henhouse, she had a bounce in her step. She wore an apron with a four-yard wraparound to it. A towel of the same linen atop her head created a beehive turban. Well off by most standards, her clothes marked her as somebody special. She had well-soled shoes on her feet, and this told Daniel, along with the carriage parked out front, that there were special goings-on at the house this evening. Probably the servant wore her best dress, her favorite apron, and her only shoes.

As the woman moved back toward the door from which she'd come, Daniel began to formulate a plan. He reached into his gunnysack and tore open the jar of lampblack. The greasy, pigmenting cream the colonel's people had collected from burning oil lamps was normally used to mix with paints, but tonight it would paint Daniel. He began to smear it across his face like soap, blessing his good luck in having picked it up instead of another jar of molasses. Within minutes, his entire face, neck, nose, ears, eyelids, hands and arms were sufficiently blackened. Shortly, he heard the kitchen door scream shut on its hinges, the heavy servant having returned to her duties there.

He looked up to see the man at the henhouse locking him out of that possibility. But now he had a backup plan. With one bold move, he stood and stepped out of the forest and into the farmstead life. Trying to be casual, he walked easy so as not to arouse suspicions. He passed several of the men working about the place without drawing any attention. In a moment, he stood below a window on his way to the kitchen door where he proposed to beg for scraps, pretending to be one of the boys from the slave quarters. From the open window, he heard a voice that sounded familiar, someone talking about his travels in the wilds of Borneo.

A female voice asked, "May I pour you some more of my elderberry wine, Major Splitshot?"

"Why, don't mind if I do, Mrs. Blainy," came the hearty answer.

Blainy! Daniel wanted to shout. How had he arrived at the farmhouse of William Blainy? Now Daniel knew he must get in and out quickly, before George Penny might catch up to him. He stole a glance at the surrounding woods. George might be out there now, staring right at him from some hiding place among the reeds or bushes or boulders.

"I have not met with such warm hospitality since my visit to Burma," came the strangely familiar voice from inside the house. "Except of course in my own beloved Louisiana! You are, Mr. and Mrs. Blainy, the most gracious of hosts, indeed."

Mrs. Blainy twittered in response like a bird. Mr. Blainy said, "Why, thank you, major."

Daniel inched toward the side porch and kitchen door. *In and out,* he kept telling himself, climbing the steps and knocking timidly at the door.

The door was thrown open, but the light from the kitchen was blocked by the great presence of the black woman Daniel had earlier seen. She looked so much bigger up close, he thought, with her ladle in her hand, her eyes staring down at him.

"Lord, child," she cried out, "you know we ain't got time for nobody here tonight what with the massa entertaining! Now get yourself on back down to your quarters where you..." but she stopped herself in mid-sentence, staring harder and saying, "I know all the children on this place, and you ain't one of ours, child. Whereabouts you come from?" She scanned the woods all around as if the answer lay there.

Daniel piped up, saying, "My name's Effram, ma'am."

"Efram? But what're you doing here all alone? Are you alone?"

"Yes'm."

"Then whose rustling in them bushes yonder?" She pointed, and Daniel turned to see Samuel, the runaway catcher's dog, amble over to him, nudging his hand.

"Alone, huh?" she asked.

"'Cept for my dog, yes."

"What you here for?"

"Hungry and looking for some eggs, maybe a scrap of bread and water."

"You ain't no runaway is you?"

"No ma'am."

"Then where's your home, boy?"

"I was charged to come here, to Mr. Blainy, ma'am."

"Charged?"

"Bought and paid for in St. Louis, ma'am, and told I had to make it here on foot, as he didn't at the time have enough money to pay my coming up with him on the steamboat. I had my dog for help, and Massa Blainy say anyone hereabouts could tell me how to get to his place."

"Why, that man—" she began, her face darker now. "He put you on the road like that, all alone, without nobody but that hound to help you get here? That's the most terrible story I ever heard! Where's your mam and your pap, boy?"

"Mam and pap're known for being good for their word and good walkers, so Mr. Blainy didn't think nothing of putting me on my own, and my pap, he was the walking-est man alive."

"Was. Was, you say? You poor child, you done lost your pap!"

"Yes'm, to the fever. Caught it whilst working the fields one fall when the crop come in with a blizzard. Overseer worked him dead, mam always said." Daniel warmed to the story.

"And your mammy? Where she be? Don't you go telling me she died of the fever, too. I know the Lord's more merciful than that. Ain't hardly a child around here with both parents alive and together, but every one of 'ems got at least one parent, and those that don't, they got me."

"Mammy was sold downriver with the others." Daniel turned his blackened face downward.

"Oh, God, what they do in St. Louis to people. When You going to end this kind of life for us?" She then bent over Daniel and hugged him so tightly his breathing stopped. While in her embrace, he felt guilty over the lies he'd had to tell, along with the lampblack disguise over his naturally dark skin.

"Your mammy done the right thing, getting you sold North 'stead of South, Effram, honey. Like to broke her heart, I know, parting with your sweet soul. Now it's as though she sent you directly to me, and in that spirit you're mine. I won't never let no harm come to you, ever."

"Thank you, ma'am," he timidly replied.

"You just calls me Daisy, honey. Now come on in and let's find some vittles for your tummy."

As they entered the well-lit kitchen, Daisy told Daniel about having lost her own son, "About your age and build, Effram, when I lost him. When he left me. It's like, in a way, his coming back, how you just showed up on my doorstep."

By the minute, Daniel's guilt grew greater and greater, but all thought of it vanished when someone shouted, "Daisy! Who's that with you?" Daniel saw a young, thin black house servant studying him now as he attempted to shoo Samuel back out the door.

Daisy said, "You just let that brave little dog come inside here too, Effram. We'll manage to feed him and you, promise."

"Effram!" shouted the thin house servant whose voice could shatter glass. "That's a funny name."

"Don't you go making fun of the boy, not what they calls you, Sissy. Besides, this boy's done trooped here all the way from St. Louis, so don't bother him. He's lost his pap to fever and his mammy to the auction block and plantation South, so be nice, you hear?"

"Just thought Effram's a big name for such a little boy." Perhaps nineteen or twenty, Sissy wrapped an arm about Daniel and said, "I'm downright sorry about your mam and your pap, Effram."

Daniel shrugged. In the light, he felt it best to say as little as possible and to draw no attention to himself. He kept his eyes averted.

Sissy guided him to a chair at the table and said, "I'll get you a mess of greens, taters and bean soup, Effram."

"You just stop that, Sissy! This boy's having what massa is having tonight; he ain't eating like the rest of us on the farm. It's roast turkey, kidney pie and a slice of pumpkin pie."

"And why's he eating better'n us?"

"He ain't just come up from the quarters! He walked here plum from St. Louis, maybe a hundred mile! All by himself with that dog of his."

Sissy whistled and looked at Effram with newfound respect. "That's some show of loyalty to Massa Blainy, ain't it? Another boy your age might've just kept on going, Effram, like your boy, George done, Daisy."

Daisy banged pots and pans at the mention of her son's name. "I told you, Sissy, I don't never want to hear that runaway's name mentioned in my presence again, ever!"

"Runaway or not, he's still your son!"

Daniel watched Daisy's big shoulders heaving up and down with the movement of her knife where she sliced turkey and bread for him. In a moment, a plate filled with food sat beneath Daniel's nose, but he could see that Daisy had been crying. "Eat," she ordered.

Daniel ate greedily while Daisy spoke to Sissy. "When I see Master Blainy next, I'm going to give him a piece of my mind."

"No you won't," replied Sissy.

"Better stop me, 'cause I'm going to light into him good! Making this young'un come all this way while he's straddling a steamboat!"

"Go on with you, Daisy. You know you won't say a word."

"I'll have my say."

Daniel prayed Sissy was right. While his plan seemed to be working wonderfully now, any attack on the master by Daisy over his wild story could prove his unmasking. *Then what? Do people get into trouble for masquerading as slaves? Has anyone ever done such a foolish thing?*

He knew he must get out of this situation as quickly as possible. He didn't want to bring calamity to anyone here. He knew the longer he stayed, the deeper Daisy would become involved with Effram She'd already appointed herself Effram's guardian angel. Her unquestioning concern made him realize how easily black families were torn apart, lives ruined. Daisy might have to live the rest of her life never to see or hear from her son again, never to know if he were alive or dead.

Having never known his own parents, Daniel tried to imagine the kind of life that could be so bad to force a boy his age into the life of a runaway, to leave behind every face and every place he had known.

Samuel greedily ate the table scraps thrown him. Daniel knew the slave catcher must be just the other side of the door, waiting for him to come out. He had to escape from Daisy's kitchen as soon as possible, but when he did, he'd run right into the clutches of Mr. Penny.

The door to the dining room burst open and in stepped Mr. William Blainy, white haired and tall, a long bone-handled cane gripped in his hand. He pointed with the cane as he shouted, "Daisy, what is all the delay? For goodness sakes, woman, we have the major waiting dinner, and you're feeding dogs and children in here? Where are your senses? Why isn't our table set?"

Mrs. Blainy followed, equally aghast, shouting, "Do you want Major Splitshot to think ill of this house? Is that your plan? Do you have a plan, Daisy May Blainy? And Sissy, are you daft, too? Don't just sit there like a fool! Help bring the platters in, and you, boy!" she shouted to Daniel, "Get up! Get up and help your elders!"

The Blainys left as abruptly as they had arrived, their hands empty. Sissy began lifting platters, and she followed the Blainys into the dining room. Daisy, her eyes fuming, said, "Best we do as massa says, honey. You ever serve a table before?"

"No'm, and I'm afeared to try."

"Effram, you can do anything you set your mind to, boy." She smiled as she said this, and she added, "Now here, take this turkey platter into the other room. May's well baptize you quick and get it done."

"But Miss Daisy, I—"

"Never you mind. I'll be right behind you. Now go on ahead."

Daniel didn't want to go into the other room. Someone was bound to see through his disguise. He hesitated before the door.

Daisy nudged him, saying, "Go on, honeypot, ain't nothing to it. Just put the turkey on the table and skee-daddle on out of the master's sight as quick as you can."

Daniel heaved a sigh of resignation, almost turning the turkey over where he stood, but Daisy quickly righted it for him, saying, "Careful, Effram...careful!"

As Daniel put his weight against the door, he heard Daisy mutter under her breath, "Lordy, wish Ichabod was here. Mr. Blainy done turned mean these past few days—angry at Ichabod, angry all the time. Something's up. Only wish I knew what's up."

Sissy passed them as they entered, and hearing Daisy's last words, she whispered, "Old Ichabod knows what's up, but he ain't saying."

"Ichabod don't keep no secrets from me," Daisy whispered back, ushering Daniel and the turkey through the door. She carried a loaf of baked bread and a bowl of stewed squash.

CHAPTER TEN

A SLAVE'S WORST FEAR

There was lively conversation and a sizeable amount of food spread across the Blainy table. The dining room and house reminded Daniel of Colonel Halverston's place: roomy, built when craftsmen took pride in their work. Large, studded beams crossed the ceiling, extending out into the kitchen. A stone fireplace crouched in the great hall. It must have once been the scene of fashionable dances and parties, but just as George Penny had reckoned that the colonel had fallen on hard times, so did Daniel reckon the same for the Blainys due the age and condition of the paint on the walls, the furniture, and Mr. and Mrs. Blainys' clothes.

Mrs. Blainy's lavender and lace dress designated her the matron of the mansion. A spindley woman, she wore too much powder and makeup, giving her a scarecrow appearance, her face sack-white. She constantly twittered as she spoke, and she seldom stopped speaking and squeaking. She now rested her chin on her knuckles, blinking eyelids birdlike at the man who sat on her right. Like her, he talked non-stop, despite the food in his mouth.

At Mrs. Blainy's other side sat two boys, about seventeen and eighteen years old. The boys ate as much as the adults talked, so they paid Daniel no attention. Next to Mr. Blainy sat a girl, thin and pale, perhaps fourteen. Her eyes followed Daniel. She wasn't talking, and she wasn't studying her plate as the boys were. Instead she studied Daniel. Daniel felt her eyes trailing him even as he brought in the turkey. He sensed that she knew he didn't belong. Did she also know he was white? Or did she just wonder where this new black boy had come from? Placing the turkey in the middle of the table, Daniel began to sweat, stealing another look at the little girl. She wore her black hair in a bun. Her stare reminded Daniel of a milky-eyed, sick cow. Her skin was pale white and pink.

"Auntie, Auntie!" she called out to Mrs. Blainy, while staring a hole through Daniel.

Daniel's hands began to shake. He was certain the girl meant to expose him. But Mrs. Blainy paid no mind whatsoever to her niece, so taken was she with Major Splitshot. Daniel shot the major a quick glance. His voice sounded so familiar. The man wore a long, white beard, spectacles and a mustache. Daniel didn't recognize him.

Then Mr. Blainy grabbed Daniel by the wrist and declared, "I'll show you exactly what we're talking about, major. Look closely at this here boy of mine." He turned Daniel to face the major, and added, "Boy, tell the major here your name and age."

"Ahh, ahh, Effram, aged seventeen, maybe."

"Effram what, boy?"

Daniel knew that slaves had to take on their masters' names, so he barked out with pride, "Blainy, sir. Effram Blainy."

Mrs. Blainy beamed and said, "See how well brought up this boy is, how respectful and behaved?"

Daniel felt ill at ease, and he saw the little girl grin wide with pleasure at his discomfort. The two boys stared briefly at him now as well, but they went back to their food. Meanwhile, Daisy stood nearby, secretly seething and worrying about Effram. The major complimented the Blainys by responding with, "Well, young Effram here done a fine job waiting table."

Daniel studied the major's features closer now, the size and shoulders recalled any number of fat men he'd known or met, but the eyes, the brow, the rose red cheeks belonged to Sheriff Brisbane. Daniel masked his own features well, averting his widening eyes before Brisbane might know that he knew of his game. *No wonder the voice was so familiar. But what's the sheriff doing here in disguise as a major?*

Mr. Blainy patted Daniel on the shoulder the way a man pats his favorite dog, saying, "This boy's like all the rest. Been with me since the day he was born, and each of my Negroes are as faithful and as trustworthy as the day is long, Major."

The little niece stuck her tongue out at Daniel. He dared not return the gesture. Instead, he bowed and backed from the room. Returning to the kitchen, he found Daisy and Sissy had been joined by a thin, white-haired old man with a tuft of a white mustache over his lip and a pair of wire-rimmed spectacles before his eyes. He, like Daisy and Sissy, was dressed in his best clothes—a black vest with no buttons, a beige linen shirt with a red handkerchief in its pocket, and cotton pants as green as grass. The old man was lean, stoop-shouldered, perhaps seventy years old. Yet his step and movements were spry. He paced back and forth, worrying some problem out in his head.

Daisy was asking, "You gonna tell us what all this hoop-de-la with that major man in there is all about Ichabod, or not?"

The old man, not wanting to answer, pointed to Daniel instead and asked, "Who's boy is this'un? I must be getting old. Can't put him with a name."

"You knows very well who Effram is!" yelled Daisy. "Effram, the boy just bought by massa and told to hoof it here from St. Louis!"

"St. Louis? Just now bought? Walked all this way?"

"Never you mind about Effram. He's here now, and I got him under my apron, so you just tell us about this major man in there." She pointed to the dining room door.

"I don't know what's come over Massa Blainy and the missus," replied Ichabod, shaking his white head. "Done got mean, I reckon. Ain't the same man no more. Acts like we all a big burden. Money coming short since the night that steamer went down with all hands and his cargo aboard. All them crop bundles, a year's worth of picking. And now he goes off and buys this boy, Effram? Just when he's talking sell everything."

"Sell? Everything?" replied Daisy as Sissy clutched at her apron.

"Selling? We be sold again?" asked Sissy.

Ichabod slowly nodded.

"All of us?" asked Daisy.

"I only just found out for sure, Daisy," he said. "I couldn't believe it, 'cause this here major, he's from... from..."

"Deep South, Louisiana," finished Daisy, sitting down heavily now, her face falling, her hands flat on the table.

Ichabod put a hand on her shoulder, saying, "That's the hardest part to believe, that Mr. Blainy would sell us downriver."

Sissy added, "But Mr. Blainy always give his word he wouldn't do that."

Daisy added, "I even heard him bragging to other white folks that no matter what comes, he ain't never going to sell his black people down the river. Up, maybe, but never down!"

Daniel watched a tear come into the old man's eye as the man heaved a sigh. "Mr. Blainy's hit hard times for sure. Lost all his money on the market. Already sold almost all his livestock, 'cept us, and you know how he feels about that prize sheep that won blue ribbon last year."

"Hoof and mouth, come take those sheep out," cursed Daisy.

Sissy added to the curse, saying, "After we're gone, come and take this home!"

Ichabod protested, "Stop that kinda talk now, you hear? Man's crops are under the Mississippi. What else he gonna do?"

"You listen to yourself, Ichabod! Making excuses for the massa selling us South. There ain't no excuse big enough."

"Daisy," he began, "you and me, we been together so many years. I was with you in Mississippi when your man died of the cholera, and I was sold with you and that lot down to the lower Arkansas country where you lost your boy, George."

Daisy wiped her tears. "Have you told the others?" Daniel thought her the strongest woman he had ever met.

"No," he replied softly. "Wanted to tell you first, old woman."

"Don't know if I like being told this kind of news first."

Ichabod closed the door noiselessly when he left, but Daisy jumped to her feet and trailed after him. On the porch, she hugged the old man tightly against her and asked, "When?"

"Tonight, tomorrow. I can't say. Depends on his deal with the major."

Ichabod walked off toward the slave quarters, bent, looking beaten. Daisy, Sissy and Daniel watched him until he disappeared. Daniel also looked toward the woods for any escape route; at the same time, he wanted to tell Daisy and Sissy, they couldn't be better off, that the major was really Sheriff Brisbane, and that they would be boarding the Underground Railroad. But Daniel couldn't give up the truth without giving himself away.

Just then, Daisy wrapped her arms around him. "Don't you worry none, Effram. You poor child. Just got traded twice in one breath, and your feet ain't hardly touched Blainy soil. But I'm here to protect you, honeypot."

⌛ ⌛ ⌛

Only an hour later, Daniel stood in the pitiful one-room slave house where Daisy lived. The place reminded him of the cave that he and Joe Grier played in back in Hannibal. Daisy slept on a straw-tick bed, beneath walls of unpainted mortar and rough-hewn logs. The earth the cabin had been built over served as its floor. The place smelled of damp earth and cooking odors, stale and trapped air. "We've had it too easy for too long here," Daisy was saying. "Going to be spoiled for real work down South."

Daniel now felt sick with worry over staying too long, attempting escape, and possibly being sold into slavery to the Deep South as Effram. His only relief came when he reminded himself that Sheriff Brisbane was in the business of helping slaves get free to the north, so the situation wasn't as hopeless as everyone thought. He only wished he could tell Daisy what he knew, but he feared it would spoil the sheriff's carefully prepared plans for the others.

To pass the time, Daniel asked Daisy about her son, George, remarking that he had only known one George in all his life, and he turned out to be a lowdown bounty hunter.

Daisy sat now on her bed and stared through the single small window at the night sky. "My George, when he was first sold North, from Arkansas, where we all come from, my boy just upped and run off to Illinois. I thought sure he'd be caught—most runaways are."

"Not if they get on the Underground Railroad."

"You get that notion right outta your head, Effram! George always talked about the road, too, and Lord knows what come of him. One man from our farm made free, name of Henry, but he wasn't smart. Stopped short of Canada."

"Is your boy in Canada?"

"Don't know, but he got to be. I haven't heard from him in near ten years now."

"How'd this here fella, Henry, get caught?'

"Foolish is all. Stopped over to Springfield just the other side of the river in Illinois. There he let himself be horn-swaggled by one of his own people there!"

"I know a man who runs down his own kind, using a hound and a long gun," said Daniel.

As if not hearing him, she went on, saying, "Henry feared every white man's eye, feared he'd be found and dragged back. Massa paid top dollar for a returned slave, and Henry had seen himself described in a bill someone had thrown away. He took his trembling fears to a relative who give him bad advice, telling him to see a black woman who could tell his fortune. The fortune-teller learned everything there was to learn about Henry from Henry. After casting a protective spell over the boy, she sent him home, telling him not to worry no more."

"I reckon the spell didn't work, huh?'

"No, but the fortune-teller and her husband did. They sent a letter to Massa Penrose—he be our master down to Arkansas. Meaner'an a Blainy by four quarter mile. Anyway, the madam fortune-teller told Penrose the exact spot where Henry could be found, and they collected a reward on him."

"Where's Henry now?"

"Next cabin, two down. Lucky he didn't get sold downriver, but Master Penrose sold the lot of us to Blainy that year, and he threw Henry in, knowing him to be trouble. He tries to run off from here every other Christmas."

Sissy stood now in the open doorway and said, "That Henry story ain't near as good as the one about your boy, Daisy."

"That boy shamed me, Sissy."

"Ain't no shame in making free!"

"Is, if you got the trust of the massa, and you got the run of the place and the whole county. Is, if you're given special freedoms and you abuse 'em!" Daisy glared at Sissy, feeling the anger of right on her side. She then turned and explained to Daniel, "George was born a throw-back, a sickly runt, and with his awkward self, all he did was get in the way, in the kitchen, in the barn, in the henhouse...just hobbling and stumbling over everything. The boy was...worthless, but I loved him just the same."

"Worthless? That ain't no way to talk about your only son, Daisy." Sissy now sat alongside her older friend. The soft light of the candle played over her thin features, and she looked kinder and prettier here than in the kitchen.

"Truth is truth," declared Daisy. "Massa couldn't get a dime for that hanger-on, that castoff. Shoulda culled him at birth like the bad apple he was. Should've seen he was a bad seed."

"She's just talking," Sissy told Danaiel. "Angry 'cause George didn't tell her what he was planning. He just upped and did it."

"I become so proud of that boy by then," muttered Daisy, fending off tears. "He'd just begun to make something of himself. The boy begun to learn from that kindly old man, a Yankee come down from Connecticut to work for Mr. Penrose, and he teached George until there weren't no more to teach the boy. Massa Penrose took notice and begun to brag on the boy, and he hired him out to all the surrounding farms."

"George learnt to fix anything, and when that old Yank died, the massa give George his job," added Sissy.

"Was alone too much," said Daisy. "Too much time alone gets a man to thinking too much; can't be good for nobody."

Sissy continued, saying, "Next thing you know, Massa Penrose give George a horse and wagon, had him going all over the county, sometimes into the next county. George could fix anything for anybody at the lowest price. Mr. Penrose turned him out for profit."

"Smartest boy anyone ever seen," muttered Daisy, a prideful look flashing across her face.

"Always with that tool box of his, always working on some busted thing or other," added Sissy. "Always coming home with his pockets full with money for Massa Penrose."

Daisy smiled openly now and said, "He was going down to all the river towns, making boats and canoes for people."

"Tell Effram how he come and go all the time, anytime," urged Sissy. "How he was more free than any of us."

"He surely had the least reason of any of us to run off!"

"But he did have reason; we all got reason."

"Escape was so easy for him; he might've done it any time, and might've give me some warning. He learnt ciphering from that Yankee man, learnt how to tell time, to read and write some. He was my smart boy by then."

"Took sand for him to run off. I'm glad he made free. Glad for any black person who finds freedom any way he or she can."

"You going to make some man happy some day, Sissy." Daisy turned to Daniel and explained further, saying, "My George, he didn't get on with the other Blacks when he was a child, 'cause he couldn't work the fields like the others, and so he got easy kitchen and barn work. Other black boys hated him for it, felt jealous. All the special treatment coming from the mechanic and then with Massa Penrose hiring George out, relations between him and the other boys only got worse."

"Poor fella even slept alone in the barn nights to keep from getting into fights down at the quarters," added Sissy. "Time he turned fifteen, he become the most valuable slave on the place, maybe in the county."

"How'd he make free?" asked Daniel.

"Don't you go getting no ideas, Effram!" warned Daisy.

Sissy blurted out, "Darned if he didn't make a canoe for a man who lived along the river, and then and there he decided to use it for himself, for his own escape. No one ever heard from him again."

"I like that style," said Daniel, grinning.

"After that, Massa Penrose never put trust in another black soul again. He never let none of his slaves learn to cipher, read, write or use a tool. 'Fraid my George left us worse off than we were."

Sissy shouted, "He couldn't just ask massa for permission, now could he? And when did massa teach any of us anything, including George? It was that Yankee mechanic taught George nights in the barn. Daisy, you got to be proud of that boy of yours."

Daisy glared now into Sissy's eyes. "I might be, girl, if I knew he was...he was safe and alive and free. We don't hear nothing; we don't know nothing. For all we know, the Devil done took that boy."

Sissy's triumphant look faded. She pushed herself into Daisy's arms, hugging the big woman. Daniel took the opportunity to inch toward the open door, and in a moment he stood outside on the plank walk, breathing in the cool night air, a little shaken but anxious now to take his leave from the Blainy plantation and life as Effram. A look at the woods told him to run.

CHAPTER ELEVEN

THE NIGHT MARCH

Daniel took a step toward the woods, toward escape, when a fifty-foot bonfire exploded into life ten or eleven feet out, in front of Mr. Blainy's house. The fire lit up Mr. and Mrs. Blainy, Major Splitshot—and several armed white men, strangers to Daniel until his eyes fell on Lem. They appeared to be men recruited from the posse that Daniel had seen. The sheriff was running out his game, a serious, unlawful but humane game. As an agent for the Underground Railroad, he could be hanged for swindling Mr. Blainy into surrendering his slaves to "Major Splitshot."

"Come on, Effram," said Ichabod, taking Daniel by the arm. "Massa wants every one of us up to the big house for his farewell speechifying."

"But I just been sold here just two days ago, Mr. Ichabod."

"No matter, boy. We've all been sold for this here major's check."

Ichabod held firm to Daniel until he turned Effram over to Daisy's big arms. The sound of the bonfire roar had by now alerted everyone in creation, Daniel imagined. He saw the three faces of the Blainy children laughing and pointing from the upstairs windows.

In a moment, with Daisy's hand clutching onto Daniel's, all the slaves stood with their backs to the bonfire. Each black man's shadow cast a dancing, jagged figure up the porch steps, touching the feet of the white men standing there. Mr. Blainy ushered his tearful wife inside. The slaves had huddled in one group, perhaps twenty-five in all. The sheriff, still in his best Southern-plantation-looking clothes, stood with his head slightly bowed, but his eyes ran over the crowd.

His voice so weak, Mr. Blainy could hardly form words. Daniel guessed that his heart was not in the business at hand. He kept his eyes on the slaves, until they met Ichabod's. That's when he lowered his eyes. He talked for some time about how difficult life in general was, then about the state of the nation, about the state of Missouri, and finally about his personal income. He said he wanted nothing more than to keep his family together. "Seeing some of you go—seeing all of you go—tears my heart out. There's no other way to say goodbye than to say it right out. I only hope that you all will find it in your hearts to understand that this sale of goods is for your best, and not mine. At least, this way, you will all remain together."

Daniel could tell that Mr. Blainy wanted Ichabod or one of the others to say something kindly, like, "Thank you for selling us together" or "We know it ain't what yo want, Mr. Blainy," but no one spoke up.

The slaves only stood in stark silence as the major's men lit their torches from the bonfire. The fire sent cinders up into the black sky like so many lightning bugs.

"We'll march in columns of two!" shouted Major Splitshot. "Straight for the river. My men are posted at your side, and in the rear, with orders to shoot down anyone trying an escape! So don't even get out of line! Two abreast, now! Line up!"

Daisy and all the slaves had collected their belongings, which didn't amount to much. A great deal of confusion came when they tried to pair off into twos. Several women had bawling children on each arm.

Daniel had somehow gotten free of Daisy who shouted above the others for him, calling out, "Efrram! Efrram!"

Daniel stood within two feet of the bushes when one of the guards stepped in front of him, nudging him with his long gun. "Where you off to, boy?"

"My dog done got away. I thought I saw him in there," he replied, pointing to the underbrush.

"You just leave the dog, boy. Major didn't pay for no dogs, and neither will the auctioneer."

"Auctioneer?"

But Lem didn't answer. He grabbed Daniel by the collar and tugged him back to the crowd, where Daisy glared at Lem so meanly that Daniel thought the gun would melt under her stare.

"Where'd you get off to, Effram?" she asked. "You gave me a fright."

Daniel felt Sam, nibbling now at this leg, wagging his tail. "There's your dog," Lem said and stepped away.

Soon Daniel found himself on a forced march with the whole population of plantation slaves. Daisy held tightly to him. The grass reached to Daniel's waist in places. He saw several men looking about as if they might drop into the dense grass, drop out of the march and wait for the procession to go on. Daniel saw one tall man go down, think better of it, get up and run to catch his partner. The white men carrying guns stood all around the sad parade, occasionally pointing their guns but saying not a word. Still in his major's disguise, the sheriff led the way, a torch lighting his features.

The group moved quietly except for the thrashing of the high grass as they passed and the hoot of an occasional owl. The torchlights held by the white men gave the world an eerie glow. As the band approached the river, they stepped into a dense fog. Daisy, to break the chill of the silence and the sorrowful march, began to hum and then sing a song as they moved along, and the other slaves joined in.

The sheriff rushed back from his place at the front, shouting, "Quiet down! Quiet, I say!"

The singing abruptly stopped. The sheriff now cocked his head to one side, listening. The woods swelled with fog.

Daisy began to speak to Daniel, "Why, you're just a little lost lamb, Effram, but you ain't to worry. No matter what comes, I'll see you stay with me. You keep your little honeypot mouth shut, and ain't nobody going to know you ain't my rightful son, so's we can stay together forever and ever."

Daniel didn't like the idea of taking up room on Sheriff Brisbane's Underground Railroad as extra baggage. He wanted in the worst way to tell Daisy, Ichabod, Sissy and the others that they were on the freedom trail, that they were heading north toward Canada and not south to Louisiana. He wanted to come clean, tired of the lies and his own disguise as Effram.

They stumbled out of the dense trees and thicket. Far ahead a strange light glowed. Daniel heard the slapping of the river. They'd reached the riverbank. Now they marched along the shore, always going toward the floating light ahead. Suddenly those in front of Daniel and Daisy stopped. Ahead, voices filtered back to them, and an uneasy feeling welled up among the slaves. Everyone began to fidget.

Daniel near jumped out of his skin when he heard a great noise like a sick crow or ailing loon caught in a bear trap. "Kack-kacka-kaw-kaw-kaw! Kack-kacka-kaw-kaw-kaw!"

Daniel realized though, that the noise was a signal that was now being answered by a bellowing Sheriff Brisbane. "Wack-wacka-waw-waw-waw-waw! Wack-wacka-waw-waw-waw-waw!" *He sure must seem crazy to the slaves,* Daniel thought.

The slaves now looked to Icabod. Poor Ichabod could only shake his head and throw his hands up. Having never ridden on the freedom train before, he didn't know what was happening.

In a moment, a floating light appeared and Major Splitshot's men herded everyone onto a great flatboat. Lem's torch lit the way. Daniel looked the flatboat over as it came his turn to step aboard. It was a large one with two cabins on deck, like the one he'd seen from the cave during the storm some nights back. It was like a raft that had become too big and had grown a rudder.

The sheriff's men had run the giant raft up under a bluff and tied-to at some tree trunks, dropped a gangplank across the rocks and had waited in the fog for the group. When Daniel started across the wobbly gangplank with Daisy, she almost tumbled over into the shallows. The sheriff guided those ahead into the larger of the two cabins through a black hole of a doorway.

Daniel caught Lem's boot in his backside.

"Don't you never kick my boy, Effram, ever again!" Daisy hissed, staring down Lem's long gun as she told him off.

"Come here, you, boy!" shouted Lem to Daniel.

Daniel did as instructed.

"Turn around," said Lem.

Daniel turned around, and Lem again kicked him squarely in the seat of the pants. Daniel was picking himself up off the deck when he heard Lem's grunt. He looked over his shoulder to see Lem splash into the water over the side. Daisy had sent him sailing overboard.

Several of the other guards stood around Daisy now, their guns held just under her flaring nostrils. "Inside! Inside!" they hissed. The sheriff continued moving the slaves into the dark cabin.

Daniel thought Lem was either pretty smart to pretend meanness so well, not wanting anyone to guess him an underground agent on the road, or he was one of those who worked the freedom road for money.

Once everyone had entered the dimly lit cabin, the door was locked. Only one old, weak oil lamp burned, and it seemed to be swallowing up all the air. As his eyes became accustomed to the dim light, Daniel counted fifty or more people. The damp cabin reminded Daniel of being alone in Colonel Halverston's underground cavern with a single lamp in his hand.

Daniel coughed on the stale air. Then he sat on the floor next to Daisy. Ichabod remained the only person standing. He moved about the other people who had already been on board when the Blainy party arrived. One man was almost hidden in deep shadows, and Daniel realized that his arms were over his head, held there by chains!

No one else had chains on. The picture didn't sit right with what Daniel knew of Sheriff Brisbane's freedom operation. *Why would they chain a man they were taking to Illinois and on to Canada?*

Daniel strained to see around Ichabod, who was cautiously asking the stranger, "Why they got you bound up in chains, mister? Why you the only one of us mistreated? What'd you do to deserve this?"

"My name is George," the man answered. "And you are Ichabod Penrose, more lately Ichabod Blainy—minister, consoler, healer of your people."

"My Lord, it's you, George! It really is you!"

"My mother, is she with you?" asked George as Daisy pushed past Daniel.

Ichabod turned to Daisy, saying, "Daisy, it's your George. It's your boy!"

"Lord, is it true?" Daisy replied, now reaching the broken man and hugging him.

"Momma, it's me, George. It's true. I come back to find you."

"You done that much," said Ichabod.

"Blessed be to Jesus, it is you, George!" cried Daisy, and then she added, "What did those evil mens do to you, son!"

Daniel now knew that George Penrose, Daisy's son, was none other than George Penny, the runaway slave catcher! Daniel inched back into the darkness, trying to figure out what had happened.

At the same instant, everyone else on the barge, seeing how Daisy and her son had been reunited, began to search the cabin, calling out names and asking after lost loved ones. One female voice asked over the noise, "Anybody here know my momma? Her name be Miss-ress Dooley, Mary Dooley."

A chorus of other questions followed. "Anyone know Jasper Gibbs?"

"May Tyler?"

"Tip Walker?"

"Israel Horton?"

"Holly Masters?"

Answers came back in shakes of the head and grunts of no. Persistent, another man asked, "My brother, Levin, he be here?"

Aunt Rea lives on a farm near-bouts here someplace," came another woman's voice in the dark. "Used so to love my Aunt Rea, so much it hurt. Fine cook she was. Wilmott be her slave name."

Daniel's heart sank as the slaves began to call out news of their relatives in hopes of reunion. Next they tried to match people by locales, trying to use geography. "Anyone from around St. Louis way?" Some found each other and spoke quietly together. Others shut down. Some cried. Still others continued calling out more names of towns, rivers, farms, former masters until the search for common ground died.

Now, Daniel had another secret to keep from Daisy. He felt that knowing that her son had grown up to become a bounty hunter of runaway slaves would surely kill her.

CHAPTER TWELVE

ABOARD THE WRONGWAY RAILWAY

"I could have made for Wisconsin and then on to Canada, but I stopped on the Illinois side and sank my canoe," George was telling Daisy, Ichabod, a wide-eyed Sissy and a number of others gathered around him as the flatboat moved swiftly and surely over the water now. The keelboat now had found deep water. As George told of his escape from slavery, his mother dabbed at his wounds, whimpering and muttering at what she saw.

"I climbed that hill across from Hannibal, Momma, the one you always pointed at when we'd go by there on the trading boat Mr. Penrose run in at Hannibal. Remember how you told me there was a man lived on that north point on the ledge, where he put out a light every night for runaways?"

"I only told a story that was passed from mouth to mouth. It was more hope than truth, son."

"But it proved true, Momma," he replied. "Take a good look at my boots. They were special made for me by Mr. John Fairfield, the man who owns that house on the hill." Daniel watched as the others drank in all of George's stories, and he again noticed the man's smooth ochre skin, the point of his nose, high cheekbones and keen eyes, just as alert as his dog's. Daniel wondered for a moment what had become of Sam.

"Who is this Fairfield?" asked Ichabod, who had examined George's boots, having slipped the left one off, searching out how it helped his clubfoot.

"John Fairfield has helped more runaways on the Underground Railroad than any man in these parts, Ichabod."

"You mean he's a slave stealer?"

"No, an abolitionist."

"Abo-who-linist?" asked Daisy.

"Abolitionist, momma. A man who don't believe in slavery no more than in drowning a dog, don't believe in slavery of no kind, nowhere on earth, a man who is in a war to abolish all slavery in the United States. Mr. Fairfield says the Constitution of the United States says every person is supposed to be free. Says that's what the country was made for in the first place."

Ichabod shook his head, saying, "But Missouri law says abolition is against the law."

"They passed a bad law in Congress," he explained, "called the Fugitive Slave Act, part of a big compromise to keep it all from coming down to a war between North and South, part of the Missouri Compromise. But Mr. Fairfield and a lot of others like him say there ain't no compromising with sin and the Devil, and that slavery is the work of sinners and Satan working through men."

"Then Missouri law...Missouri Compromise laws, they go against the law the country was founded on?" asked Daniel, having listened intently to George's explanation.

George stared for a moment at Daniel as if trying to decide who he was, but then he quickly added, "That's right, boy. Mr. Fairfield believes the Fugitive Slave Law goes against the Bill of Rights, the Constitution and Christian charity—all the principles that made America."

"That's mighty fine specifying," said one powerful-looking black man who'd inched closer to hear it all, "but it don't get us free, brother." This man wasn't a Blainy slave but had taken a beating himself and had come to the barge with another group.

George ignored the other man's glare, and added, "Mr. Fairfield says the wrongful law will have a good result, because no man can straddle the fence no more, because no one who holds strong beliefs about freedom can abide all the compromising and bargaining that Congress has been doing. No man worth his salt can compromise with slavery, Mr. Fairfield says."

"Mr. Fairfield says, Mr. Fairfield thinks..." mocked the big man standing over George now, his teeth set. "So where's all the white Mr. Fairfields now? What good are they to us? We be all sold South into hell!"

"I got a plan," muttered George.

The other man only laughed. "You? You with yourself all chained up, you got a plan?" He sauntered off to tell the joke to his friends. Daniel heard one of them call him Grady.

"How come you to stop in Illinois and not go clean on to Canada, son?" asked Daisy.

"Cold in Canada, Momma," joked George, "besides, I saw a chance to learn the ways of the road with Mr. Fairfield and his sons. There's no end to the knowledge in the man."

"The road?" asked Sissy, whose eyes never seemed to leave George.

"The Underground Railroad, girl. Business on it is higher now than at any other time, thanks again to the Fugitive Slave Act passed by Congress in 1850. Riled a lot of people for the government muckety-mucks in Washington to tell them they had to return a runaway slave to his master, no matter if he is on free soil or not. In a backward way, we kinda got the law on our side this time, popular opinion being so against it and all."

"Who turn't you in, son?" asked Daisy, as if she would kill whoever it had been.

"How'd they catch you?" asked Ichabod.

"Is the major taking you back to Massa Penrose, George?" asked Sissy.

"Major? What major? Who's the major?" he replied, confused.

Ichabod explained how they came to be on the barge, about how Blainy had sold them all to a Major Splitshot. Daniel bit his lower lip, deciding it high time he do some explaining of his own by exposing the truth. "The major ain't no major but a sheriff," he pronounced.

Daisy stared at Daniel, asking, "What you saying, Effram?"

"Sheriff?" asked Ichabod.

"Sheriff of Hannibal," said George, helping Daniel out, winking at him to let him know his disguise hadn't fooled him.

"And I got something else to tell you, Daisy, Mrs. Penrose."

"I know you do, honey," said Daisy. "Knowed it for some time, just after seeing you put that turkey on the table. Didn't have sense enough to put it before the master. No black boy would ever make that mistake."

"Then you know?" asked Daniel

Ichabod said with sudden revelation, "This boy's white!"

Sissy stared, amazed, saying, "Effram, you ought be ashamed. You do this all the time? Dress up Black, pass yourself off as a slave to be fed?"

"No'm, not a lot, and my name's not Effram but Daniel, Daniel Webster Jackson, and I got good news for you, too. This here ain't an auction block situation you all are in, but I have it on good authority that Sheriff Brisbane is running you all north, north to freedom, and this here is a freedom train boat."

"That don't figure right, Daniel," said George. "It was Sheriff Brisbane who beat me near unconscious and locked me up here. Told me straight out he was going to hide the fact of my clubfoot and my freedom papers from the auctioneer in St. Louis and get plenty of money on me. Said if I didn't hold my tongue at the sale, he'd cut it out."

"I don't understand the sheriff at all, George." Daniel told the story of how Brisbane had helped the runaways who had fled through Daniel's camp, "Helped those runaways just like Old Billy and Colonel Halverston did. I saw it with my own eyes! He's an agent on the road, just like...like..."

"Like I am?" asked George. "Daniel, you been turned around and wrong about me all this time, and now you got turned around and wrong about the sheriff."

"You're an Underground Railroad agent?"

"I am."

"And the sheriff ain't?"

"Look around you, Daniel. He's helped himself to a lot of other people's slaves in one way or another, but not so's he can help anyone but himself. I know how a Railroad line heading north is run, know every line from this area and which way it goes and how it's handled and who's behind it. Knew about Old Billy's operation, didn't I?"

"Yeah, but—"

"Been with Mr. Fairfield for near ten years now, and we never got a lick of help from the law in Missouri nor Hannibal. If you think on it for a minute, Daniel, you'll realize this boat ain't pointed north."

Daniel gave this serious thought and feeling. *George's right. The speed at which we're moving tells the story. The lumbering barge's being swept south on the current.*

"Hear any grunting, cursing or fighting outside on deck?" asked George.

Again George was right. If Brisbane's gunmen had turned into oarsmen, heading against the current, they'd be sweating and cursing the river by now for sure, but not so much as a footfall could be heard beyond the cabin walls. The only sound against the barge remained the river itself, pushing it easily downstream. "Downriver," Daniel said in a near shout. "We're moving too easy, too fast and silent."

George and Daniel's discussion had gathered a large crowd around them. The man named Grady and a friend he called Eben stood with fiery eyes, listening to every word. Daniel now recognized Grady and Eben as two of the slaves who'd run through his camp the other night. The one called Eben had been their leader, the man who had given over his trust to Sheriff Brisbane when the others had wanted to bolt in another direction.

"He must have quite a counter-Railroad running," said George.

"Counter-Railroad?" asked Daniel.

"An unofficial Underground Railroad, but one running south instead of north to freedom," George explained, "a wrongway Railway! Going farther south."

"But why?"

"Money, of course."

Daniel shook with the thought. George said, "Sheriff said he could get five hundred dollar easy for me. Told me so when he caught me by surprise again. Didn't want to hear about trouble with my clubfoot anymore, not seeing how far I'd come on it."

"I can't believe the sheriff is so low-down," said Daniel.

"Greed, Daniel."

This didn't soothe Daniel's feelings.

"Mr. Fairfield knew this kinda thing was going on hereabouts for years, but he couldn't find out how it was done or who was behind it. Now I know, but I can't get word to Mr. Fairfield. Brisbane would be put away for life if he got caught slave snatching. He'd do anything to keep a witness like you from turning him in. That's why you have to keep to your disguise, Daniel."

"But I can't stay a Blainy slave! I'd be sold down river like...like..."

"Like the rest of us?" asked Sissy beside him, a bitterness in her voice, as though she was glad to see a white person—any white—in this predicament.

"You have to stay one of us, child, until we can figure a way to get you free without them bad men knowing," said Daisy, a warm hand on his shoulder. "Don't you worry, honey, we'll find a way. George'll think up a way, won't you, George?"

George shrugged, causing his chains to clink, and no one said anything for a long moment. Finally, Daniel asked George, "Is Judge Hatcher all mixed up in this counter-Railroad, George?"

"No, I'm pretty certain he doesn't know what his sheriff's been up to. Sherrif knows he can get away with it. Not so hard to make up your own laws when the laws the government makes are so conflicting. Brisbane was likely certain when he began his operation, which must be six or eight year ago, that he'd one day lose his sheriffing office. He wanted to use his time well, so he come up with this wrongway railway of his."

"Turned his office to bad," added Ichabod, shaking his head.

George replied, "Law's bad anyway in a slave state, Mr. Ichabod."

Daniel thought for the first time how his home state must be looked upon by the slaves imprisoned in it. He'd never thought of it as a slave state before, but he certainly felt the weight of its being a slave state now. "So you ain't really no runaway catcher, then, Mr. Penny, Mr. Penrose," began Daniel. "That was only your disguise so you could find your mother again."

"Penny is my chosen name, Daniel. Don't want to go by a slave name forced on me ever again. But yeah, you're right. I was out to catch runaways, but only so as to help them, any way I could."

"Took a lot of bravery to come back to these parts," commented Ichabod.

"Mr. Fairfield knew I wanted to find my momma, but his operation couldn't locate her until lately; come up with the name Blainy. I had worked for years in the files, watching, waiting, doing my work for the Fairfields. I become real good at writing up freedom papers to make them look authentic. Did my work at his wood mill which doubles for a hiding place on the real Underground Railroad. Then Mr. Fairfield learned how Penrose sold you all to Blainy. I then and there made up a batch of freedom papers for myself and for fifty others. I even signed the governor's signature better than he did. I done the same for hundreds of runaways come through the mill. I finally couldn't sit back no more, watching operation after operation succeed, and slaves going through all the time and not knowing how my own momma was fending. So I made my move."

"What'd you do?" asked Daniel.

"Made up them freedom papers for fifty people, and I got my bounty-hunter disguise together, making papers out on myself."

"Where's these freedom papers at now?" asked Grady, his voice gruff.

"I had them all in my buckskin pouch, but the sheriff got 'em. He knows I'm a conductor on the real Underground Railroad, and he knows he can sell those freedom papers for a handsome profit anywhere."

Daniel imagined the papers stuck into the compact buckskin pouch, recalling the night at Colonel Halverston's when George had retrieved it from a hiding place. Just behind Daniel, Grady said to George, "You was a conductor on this here railroad, you had some free man's papers, you were a free man yourself once't, but you're caught now and in chains. You ain't no better'n any one of us, now, Mr. George Penny-Penrose."

Daniel turned to the contentious man and defended George, saying, "That ain't so! George has gotta be the bravest man I ever met. And Mr. Fairfield will come for him and help us all out!"

Then Grady's friend, Eben, said, "No white man's ever been honest with a black man! If this Mr. Fairfield was honest with you, George Penrose, then why didn't he come down here to help you? Why'd you have to brave it alone? You, a runaway yourself."

George's anger flared. "Mr. Fairfield has shot other white men, defending runaways, mister! Fairfield does come down here on raids, many times, with his boys! He pretends being a doctor from Canada, sometimes a judge, a captain, or a colonel. He's got a right-smart French accent he uses sometimes, too. Got it down real good. He picks his time and place careful and uses his head!"

This caused some grumbling and thought among Grady, Eben and the others.

George continued, saying, "Mr. Fairfield turns a plan inside and out and over. He don't go rushing in like a fool, like I did. You should hear the stories this man tells, how the other white folks he fooled thinks he's so fine when he talks about Quebec and Ontario and all the great men he knows in Parliament, Washington, New York, and over to Paris, France. He knows how to use the names of every disease, and he talks on science, medicine, politics and religion, and when he helps a runaway, he's got friends, relatives, and sons from Illinois clean to Canada to see that runaway free."

"Still ain't going to be no help to you now," Grady solemnly replied.

"Maybe...maybe not. I tell you, them freedom papers are good, if we can just get 'em back."

"There's gotta be a way," Daniel said.

Ichabod turned to the others and made a pronouncement as leader of his people. All who'd come from Blainy's wanted to hear what he had to say about all these revelations. "Daisy's boy George is telling the truth. That man who purchased us didn't rightfully purchase us. He ain't no major but a sheriff from down at Hannibal. We're heading south, and this here sheriff may have it in his head to sell us to Deep South. If that happens, we'll all go in different directions, split up like culled apples."

"You just got this white boy's word on the major," objected one man in Ichabod's camp.

"That and the word of a man who ain't never cared about any of us before now," said a sassy, young girl beside this man. "That George never had any use for nobody among us before. Left us and his mammy without asking a soul to make free with him!"

"Yeah," agreed another. "Why should we believe him now?"

Daisy stormed into them all. "Ain't none of you ever cared one lick about George all his sweet life until he made free!"

Old Ichabod waved his hands, cutting the argument short, saying, "I saw the so-called major pay off all his men at the landing, just before they put the lock on the door! If he was from Louisana like he claimed and was taking all fifty or so of us all the way to his plantation in Deep South, then he'd have brought along his own armed guards."

George shouted, "This ain't going to be a long ride, just to St. Louis."

"It's plain enough we're moving south," said Daniel.

"George here hasn't any reason to lie," shouted Daisy. "And neither does this here white boy."

There was still grumbling. Ichabod held up his hands and yelled, "Use your ears!" "Do you hear a single oarsman outside yonder? You hear any oars dipping water? Any cursing."

"We're running with the water's current," added Daniel. "The sheriff and one or two of his men are aboard, and that you can believe."

George perked up considerably at this. "That's good news. Only two or three guns on us, and we're fifty strong."

"We're still trapped," Grady said sullenly.

"But we're not surrounded by so many guns we can't handle them. This puts a different light on things altogether." He went silent a moment, thinking. "Brisbane pays off all his men up front, and then they're out of it. Probably all of 'em prefer it that way. Then he and one or two others take all the real risks."

Ichabod asked, "Wonder how long he's played out this game?"

George considered this. "Good question. If there was only some way to expose him..."

"Expose him and we're free," added Daniel.

"You'll be free," replied Sissy, her lip quivering.

"Daniel, rest of us would just be turned back to Mr. Blainy, and him still with his debts and problems. He'd just sell us all over again."

"No telling what they'd do with George," added Ichabod. "I think we'd best sleep on it. Everybody's tired and wore out."

CHAPTER THIRTEEN

A DISGUISE OVER A DISGUISE

When the morning prayers and the preaching finished, everyone sang psalms until someone banged loudly on the door and yelled for them to be quiet inside.

"That sounded like Lem," Daniel said.

"Who's Lem?" asked Daisy.

"The one you threw into the water."

"Oh, yeah, that mean one."

Daisy had nursed George's wounds all day long. She'd torn her apron into strips, dampened them at the single water basin, and tied them about his head for bandages. George had stopped bleeding, and cleaned up, he looked a fair sight better. Sissy had helped in nursing George along.

"Wish we could get them chains off my boy," moaned Daisy.

Ichabod had been sitting at the wall all night and all day, sitting still and quiet until someone interrupted his thoughts. He appeared to be thinking on the situation and how best to proceed. He'd stare at nothing for the longest time, like a cat might stare at a corner in a room. Gaunt and high-cheeked, Ichabod stood some six-foot-two, so tall Daniel thought he purposely bent at the back so as to not stand over a person too much when he spoke. His clothes hung on his thin frame like a scarcrow's. Daniel thought Ichabod's hands the biggest he'd ever seen, and when he raised them in prayer it was like two flatirons being stood on end. Daisy had told Daniel how once, when Ichabod worked in the barn, a carriage, harnessed to the rafters, had fallen on him, yet he survived. That had been ten years ago. A miracle, Daisy had said.

He erupted now, saying, "I got us a plan! I done hit upon a plan."

"What plan?" asked Daisy.

"Smallpox! That's what it is, smallpox!" Ichabod shouted.

Ichabod frightened everyone in the cabin, not only by the suddeness with which he came to life, but with the fear of being trapped inside with the terrible smallpox. Smallpox meant almost certain death. People generally called it *the fever* until one hundred or more died from it, then it was proclaimed smallpox. It was a terrible superstition that everyone held to—folks didn't call it smallpox until there was nothing left to call it. By calling it the fever, it might only kill some and be on its way. Smallpox had killed Daniel's parents.

Daniel realized Ichabod was now coldly staring right into his face. Daniel feared the old man at that moment.

Daisy saw the strange look in Ichabod's eye as well, and she placed her large self between Daniel and Ichabod, showed her fist and said, "Don't you touch this child, old man! I don't care what you saw in any crazy vision in your head!"

"Smallpox!" he shouted again, still coming closer to Daniel. "Daisy, George, look close here on this boy's face! He don't look so well, not at all!" Ichabod tore out a handkerchief and with it he dabbed at Daniel's smoky, lampblackened face. "See all these spots, here and there," he continued as he dabbed at Daniel's cheeks. The spots he created were gray-white. "That's how smallpox look, and even if it don't, how many people have ever seen smallpox?" he asked.

"A disguise over a disguise," George said, smiling.

"It's a marvelous-good plan," Daniel agreed. "They hear smallpox, and they'll be something upset with their cargo!"

"They hear smallpox, and they'll throw away the key," said Daisy, putting a damper on all the enthusiasm. "Leave us all here to rot."

"Then we won't call it smallpox," said Ichabod. "We'll let them draw their own conclusions."

"You're putting a lot of faith in that white boy," said Eben from where he sat. Grady nodded in agreement.

Sissy replied boldly. "You got a better plan?"

"Ichabod," said Daisy, "I don't want this boy put in no danger."

"He's our only hope, woman."

"Daniel wants to help, momma," George added, "and he'll do just fine. Won't you, Daniel?"

"Only one thing worries me," Daniel began, hedging after thinking the dangerous plan over. "It's just that I'm not so good at disguises, as you know, and if the sheriff looks too hard at me and sees who I am, he's going to think I got aboard as the judge's spy."

"Judge's spy?" Grady asked.

"Spy?" asked Eben.

"What're you talking about, spy?" asked Sissy.

"Can't trust him," Eben said from his corner.

"It's a good plan, and Daniel's a spy for our side!" George was angry he could not get up, move around the room and bring home the plan. He finally said, "It's the only chance we got."

"I'll do it," Daniel said.

Daisy stepped from beside Daniel, and going to the fireplace in the middle of the far wall, she covered her hands with pitch pine cinders of good age. She returned open-palmed to Daniel. "You've got to do something about them earlobes first, and that hairline," she said with a motherly smile. "First chance you see to set yourself free, young man, you take it!"

Daniel felt her kind, warm fingers at his ears and covering his forehead as she smeared the pitch pine. She then looked up at Ichabod and said, "All right, finish speckling him!" She felt truly worried for Daniel.

"Then it's settled," said Ichabod. "This is how we do it. Gather round."

At one point in Ichabod's outline of the plan, Eben shouted, "Then we jump them!"

"Right," agreed Grady.

"No!" shouted Ichabod.

Eben glared at Ichabod and said, "My men don't follow you. They follows me!"

"We've got to be together on this thing," Ichabod pleaded.

"Eben, Grady," said George from where he sat, "no sudden moves while there's a gun pointed in here. There's women and children here."

"But we can take the gun away from anyone steps in here, Eben hissed."

"The sheriff carries a second gun right here," George said, pounding his fist to his chest. "A small one."

"Then we'll jump them both," Eben said.

George was fast losing his temper. "Look, Eben, that man's got our tickets home, got our papers without which it'd be impossible to make it far."

"My men and me, we don't need no papers if we got guns," shouted Eben, a fierce look contorting his eyes and mouth. "I'm so tired, man, if they killed me yesterday, I'd have to sleep another week to catch up to my soul. So, what do I care."

Grady placed a hand on Eben's shoulder as Ichabod said, "Then stay clear out of it, Mr. Eben, and give these other folks their chance to run. You had your chance, and it got you here. We're trying to get from here. Now, you're with us, or you get back in your corner over there and stay put." Eben looked around at the others. Grady pulled him away.

Daniel heard the talk all around him. He felt the uncertainty building. He heard Grady say, "We got to put our trust in a white boy?"

"All we can do is pray," said another.

"The sheriff's got all the guns. He's got the keys, and he's got them papers most of all," Ichabod told Daniel. "You're our one chance."

"Now Daniel, what are you going to do?" George asked.

"I'm to lay so still I look dead but with a twitch here and there, and moan and fret. I'm supposed to be with fever, so I'm to complain of the heat."

"We need to sweat him up somehow," suggested Sissy. "Maybe he could run around the room some."

"I got a good, warm blanket here," said a woman beside Sissy. She handed it to Daniel and he placed it over his shoulders. Madly, he began running around the room like a frightened chicken until his brow glistened.

"Now, Daisy!" Ichabod gave the signal.

Daisy went to the door, and pounded on it and pleaded, "Major! Major Splitshot! Help me, please, please help me!"

Ichabod leaned into Daniel and whispered, "Try to keep him stalled, to keep the door open for as long as possible."

"Then what?" asked Daniel.

"I don't know...making this up as I go along."

Suddenly Daisy was answered by Lem's voice: "What in tarnation's going on in there?"

"The child! He's burning up with fever!" she shouted through the door. "He's burning up with fever! Help him, please!"

Shaken, Lem answered, "I'll...I'll get the major."

In a moment, the door was thrown open, and Lem stood in the doorway, his long gun pointed in. Brisbane entered and stood over Daniel, who lay under a blanket at the far wall, acting as sick as he was afraid. He made horrible faces, hoping this would further disguise him.

"This boy looks awful!" said Sheriff Brisbane. "He looks near death, Lem."

"Oh, my God," answered Lem. "What'll we do with him?"

"Fetch him a doctor when we reach St. Louis, I reckon."

The sheriff stood up and shook his head over the boy and shrugged. He made as if to leave, saying, "We don't have no provisions on board for the sickness." He looked into Daisy's face and said, "I'm sorry. Maybe some hot soup. I'll have Lem bring a bowl around to him."

The sheriff bent over Daniel again and nodded. "All right."

Brisbane hefted Daniel and started through the door. Daniel lifted a leg and made it difficult for him to get through, but in a moment they were clear. Daniel heard George shouting, "I guess you won't get much for a bunch of slaves with smallpox, sheriff!"

Sheriff Brisbane shouted, "Smallpox!" and flung Daniel over the side of the flatboat, out into the darkness. In another second, Daniel heard the terrible report of a single shot. He swam for the rudder of the flatboat as it neared him, caught it and held on. The mournful singing inside the cabin, sad and low, told him that the escape attempt had failed and at least one man was dead. Daisy's strong voice led the mourning song, the loneliest he'd ever heard. Daniel held tight to the rudder, feeling the easy current's drag and pull under his feet, feeling cold and believing himself a failure.

The rudder was tied-to, unmanned, dragging silently behind the boat in the deep water. Daniel was able to pull himself back onto the boat. He hid amid several bales of cotton behind the cabin where the slaves were held. He saw a light in the smaller cabin over the bow where the sheriff and Lem were probably having a drink to steady their nerves—the sheriff worried he'd touched smallpox, Daniel guessed.

It seemed that the sheriff and Lem were the only two crewmen aboard. Daniel stared at the rudder again. Leaving a rudder unmanned was dangerous business. It was done in wide water, but one always took a chance letting a boat look out for itself, current or no current. Daniel wondered just how long Lem would leave it unattended. He decided to wait and see.

Daniel dozed and was awakened by the sound of something moving toward him amongst the bundles of flax and cotton. It was too dark to see, there being no moon out. Then he heard breathing. *It must be Lem, and Lem must see like a cat in the dark, staring right at me*, the boy thought.

Daniel inched back toward the rear of the boat and sat on a pile of rope. He saw Lem at the rudder, sitting calm and undisturbed, his long gun put up at his side.

Does the sheriff have another man aboard? he wondered. Suddenly Daniel was being licked across the face and crowded by Samuel.

"Hey boy," he whispered, "how did you get onboard?"

CHAPTER FOURTEEN

A FIRST STEP TOWARD FREEDOM

Daniel awoke in the dark to Samuel's frantic nudging. Lem had left the rudder again, and the smart dog had awakened him. This was Daniel's chance.

He grabbed the rope he'd used for a pillow, rushed to the rudder and pulled it as far to the right as it would go, and tied it there. He looked down the boat and saw that Lem had already gone into the sheriff's cabin, probably for coffee or something to eat. He hadn't taken his long gun, though. Daniel took it and went back into hiding amid the bales.

Daniel knew he wouldn't be firing off any gun at anyone, so he took the long gun up to the roof of the large cabin. He let the gun drop down the chimney. "Who's up there?" called Ichabod. *Thank God, Ichabod wasn't shot,* Daniel thought.

"It's me, Daniel," he whispered down.

A muffled cheer of happiness greeted him. When Lem returned to the rudder, he hit himself on the side of his head with his palm and corrected the rudder. He mumbled something to himself, then went back to the sheriff's cabin.

Daniel went again to the rudder and reset it hard to port. Then Daniel and Samuel inched their way forward, down the other side of the boat to the sheriff's cabin. A lamp burned brightly there. The window was covered with an oilcloth sash. The sheriff and Lem were sitting at the table, passing a bottle back and forth. Lem was telling the sheriff that everything was going to be all right.

"All right?" stormed the sheriff. "It won't go well for us if we put into St. Louis with smallpox aboard. And if we sell them Blacks knowing what we know, they'd skin us alive if it ever come out. I'm not talking about being skinned by the law, Lem. I'm talking about them traders in St. Louis. They can be a mean lot if they think they've been swindled."

"Maybe we should go farther down, maybe to Vicksburg? We could get eighteen hundred for a big fellow, a good sugarcane cutter."

"You mean like the one you shot?" said the sheriff angrily.

"That wasn't my fault, Henry."

"Fool," sheriff Brisbane answered, leaving Daniel unsure who was the fool, Lem or the man he'd shot. "Can't go to Vicksburg. We got to unload as soon as possible. If there's sickness on board, I don't want to go another mile with it than I have to. We sell 'em in St. Louis and we light out, for good. This game's getting too old, anyway. Nothing to keep me in Hannibal anymore. I won't be sheriff long, now that Colonel Halverston's been voted in as judge."

Daniel grinned at this new information.

"What'll we do?"

"I got a scheme hatching," said the sheriff, who began telling Lem about some place in New Orleans he wanted to visit first.

From Daniel's crouched position at the window, he could see the key ring and key to the slaves, cabin on the table between the men. *Somehow, he told himself, I must get the keys.*

Sheriff Brisbane was now holding up George's tan buckskin pouch over his head, waving it. His eyes were red from the whiskey. "We can live off these for some time, Lem. black man with enough money'd pay a hundred dollars for a set of freeman's papers."

"A hundred dollars?"

"Sure."

"No slave's got that much."

"I ain't never met a slave who didn't have something. Maybe it's a piece of jewelry, a watch or a ring, but they'll always have something. Enough of 'em get together to help one get free, and they'll come up with more than you'd believe."

Lem nodded.

The sheriff's talk jumped from the freedom papers to the Missouri Compromise, and the next minute he spoke about the Fugitive Slave Law, saying that it helped out his business a great deal. He said, "One day, I'm gonna write a letter to Congress and tell them it was a good law." As he talked, both men drank more. Lem looked as if he'd soon fall asleep. Listening to Sheriff Brisbane, Daniel also began to doze.

⧖ ⧖ ⧖

Dawn had yet to break when a terrible noise, coupled with a frightening and powerful jolt, rocked the flatboat. As he toppled over and rolled forward toward the bow, Daniel heard the people in the cabin shouting. So did Sheriff Brisbane and Lem. They'd run aground. The rudder had done it's job.

Lem and Sheriff Brisbane ran to the port side, and were leaning way over, inspecting the damage; the sheriff was swearing at Lem.

Daniel climbed quickly through the window of the sheriff's cabin and grabbed both the keys and the freedom papers. He could hear the sheriff shouting "Get to the rudder. See if there's any damage aft!"

In a second, Daniel heard Lem's report. "My rifle's been taken, sheriff! And someone's set the rudder hard to port! We've been taken!"

The sheriff peered into the trees. Everything echoed stillness. "Who?" he shouted. "How?"

"One of them smart Blacks!" Lem answered. Had to be one of them!"

"How? How, Lem?"

"I don't know how! Climbed up the chimney stack, I reckon."

"One of them's got your gun, then."

The two men looked at one another.

Daniel felt worried. It wasn't going right. The sheriff and Lem wandered back for their extra guns, and the keys. Then they'd open the slaves' cabin door and start shooting. He tried to think. The sheriff and Lem were now hotly arguing.

"Daft! Fool!" The sheriff shouted. "Wait till I tell the boys back in Hannibal how you run a barge up onto an island!"

"It's a sandbar, sheriff."

"You got eyes! This here's Forgotten Landing! We aren't no more'n a hundred miles south of Hannibal when we should be outside of St. Louis by now! And here we sit!"

"Somebody tied her hard to port, I tell you."

Forgotten Landing! Daniel was amazed. They hadn't come as far as it had felt the last two days. They must have drifted in circles most of the night. Daniel tossed the papers and the keys through the window and climbed through himself, just in time. Sam, sitting below the window outside, took the keys in his teeth and ran around to the other side of the flatboat. Daniel, holding tightly to the freedom papers, followed the dog. *I must unlock the door and get help as soon as possible,* Daniel thought. But just as they arrived at the door and Daniel tugged the keys out of Sam's mouth, Lem and the sheriff came rushing up after them.

"It's that boy! That boy of the judge's!" shouted the sheriff.

Lem leveled his pistol, readying to take a careful shot at Daniel, who stared wide-eyed at him for only an instant. Samuel lunged at Lem, knocking him overboard. Both man and dog went under.

"You!" shouted Sheriff Brisbane, stepping closer. Daniel saw that Brisbane had no gun. "Been you all along, hasn't it? Always had bad luck, but never like I've had since the day the judge made you a spy! Judge was smarter than I give him credit for. He was onto me, wasn't he? He was being clever, telling me you would be spying on Halverston when all the time you colored yourself up like a slave to spy on me! It was you I threw overboard last night! It was you with the smallpox! I'll kill you for this!"

Brisbane lunged at Daniel, who turned and raced around the flatboat. He easily stayed ahead of the sheriff, until he ran full circle, back before the locked cabin door again. As he turned the keys, he saw the sheriff point a revolver at him. He heard the revolver being cocked just as he opened the door. As he dived inside the cabin, he heard the report of the revolver, and the squawking of a frightened flock of birds.

Daniel felt himself being lifted up by Daisy's strong hands. Sissy and others were crying. Over Daisy's asking him if he were all right, Daniel heard George shout, "Quick, Daniel! Get these chains off me! Ichabod, you give me that long gun, now!" The command in his voice was so strong, no one dared object.

Daniel scrambled to his feet, fumbling for the key that might unlock George from his chains, while Ichabod rushed the rifle to George. At the same time, they all heard the sheriff just outside the door, angry and bellowing for his single deputy. "Lem! Lem! Where in tarnation you got off to?"

Daniel's eyes fell on Eben's dead body lying in one corner. Grady and his other friends were holding silent vigil. But Daniel was too busy fussing with the keys to think about this tragedy now; instead, he located the skeleton key that set George's hands free, and the big man's hands went directly to the long gun Ichabod held out to him. The chains, still locked to one wrist, clanged against the cabin walls as George stood and grabbed hold of the gun. At the same time, Ichabod warned, "I ain't so sure this the right step, George. You kill a white man, any white man, no matter what he's done, and they'll hang you for sure, freedom papers or not."

"You want to tell that to Eben over there, Mr. Ichabod?" replied George.

Sheriff Brisbane burst through the door, his revolver pointed straight at George, cocked and threatening. Meanwhile, George had drawn a bead on the sheriff as well. Now the two men held one another at bay, while everyone else flattened against the walls, praying the gunfire would not richochet.

A little smile curled across the sheriff's face as he said, "Looks like we got ourselves a Mexican standoff, Mr. Freedom Papers man."

"Don't bet on a no-account black man knowing what you mean, Massa Brisbane, sir!" George mocked. "Seeing as how I ain't never been to Mexico, I might just pull this trigger anytime. Like now!"

A shot rang out and the sheriff screamed in pain, his gun now sailing through the air. George's bullet had shattered a bone in his leg. The pain sent Brisbane to the floor, agony coursing through him. When Brisbane fell, Daniel, Grady and several of the other slaves sat on him.

George cried out, "Now, let's find out what become of the other one."

"And Sam," Daniel added.

"My dog's out there? I thought I heard Sam," replied George.

"Sam's the one knocked Lem over the side, but he fell in with him. Sam saved my life."

Daisy had rushed to Daniel. "Are you all right, child? You hurt anywhere? We thought you'd done drowned for sure last night. I become so angry with George, I saw red, taking such a fool chance with your life, but he only did what he did trying to keep Eben from getting himself killed."

Ichabod had grabbed up Brisbane's revolver from where it had fallen, and he tore a second gun, a derringer, from Brisbane's inside coat pocket. Ichabod looked ill-at-ease with a gun in his hand, and having two now, the old man appeared downright queasy. Grady and another of his band, Tom, happily took the guns from the old man.

"I wasn't hurt none. Just got wet and had to sleep cold. But Sam, he warmed me up good, sleeping against me all night."

Led by George, the group of slaves began to inch out of the stuffy cabin. George took the pouch of freedom papers from Daniel, and attached them to the chain around his own neck. He looked for Sam and Lem. He saw only Sam barking and running amid the trees lining the riverbank, turning from sun to shadow as he sped along. In his teeth, he carried tattered cloth, ripped from Lem's pants, no doubt.

George quickly surmised the craft's predicament. It had struck an oversized sandbar. Muddy sand held the flatboat in its trap. Now, George opened his arms to Samuel, the dog kicked up water as he raced through the shallows onto the sandbar and leapt onto George's chest. Everyone, save Ichabod, laughed.

Ichabod waited for the laughter to die down, then he said, "Here we are, people, Daniel says maybe a hundred mile downriver from Hannibal, stuck on a sandbar, a shot-up sheriff tied up in there and howling, a deputy on the loose, and us without no food and no plan."

Daisy came waltzing out of Sheriff Brisbane's cabin. "There's some food inside here, and if I soup it up, we can stretch it."

Sissy, hanging on George's arm, asked him, "What're we going to do now?" Everyone looked to George.

George swept them all in at a glance. "First thing, we're going to get down off this boat and push it back into the Mississippi. Second thing, we're going to turn it northward!"

Daniel found himself joining in the cheer that rose around him.

CHAPER FIFTEEN

THINK FREEDOM

The keelboat only made fair time, going against a head wind and a strengthening current that wanted to turn them southward. Rather than fight their way against the rougher waters, they'd taken the boat clear around the sandbar and through the narrow straight, going right along the unused port of Forgotten Landing. The few people there, two old men, a few Indians and their children, waved, amazed to see any traffic on their appearing and disappearing channel. It was difficult to believe that the mainland and newly created island could be attached once more. "Where y'all headed for?" shouted a tall old man who leaned on a cane.

Daniel climbed atop the cabin roof, cupped his hands, and hollered back, "Hannibal!"

"Careful of snags! You're in shallow waters!" the other old man returned with a final wave. George's first order was for the women to tend to Brisbane's leg, and his second order was for the men to put the sheriff onto the sandbar. With the sheriff trapped there with a bad leg and no one to rescue him, George figured the keelboat would have a comfortable head start.

They had moved upriver by hugging shore in the shallows, where the current did not run so much against them. Every able-bodied man and a few women took turns at the long poles and oars. Few grumbled at George's orders. They had all seen the leadership and courage he'd displayed. They had all seen Eben get himself killed.

When Eben's friends wanted revenge, George had stood firm against killing the sheriff.

Now Eben's shrouded body lay out on deck, George telling the others that as soon as they put some distance between themselves and Sheriff Brisbane, they'd put to and find a suitable place to bury Eben. They'd run all day, keeping close on the shoreline, often touching overhanging trees and snags in the shallow water. This made the work at the keels and the rudder more difficult. Some argued they ought to be moving out into deeper water, and so when darkness came with the second shift of keelboatmen, George chanced going out from shore into a stronger current. There they had remained safe from snags, sandbars and giant dead limbs.

After a time, George had the men take the boat to an outcropping of land in the bend, where they tied to some willows. They buried Eben here, with a few psalms to mark his passing, and Ichabod said a prayer. The grave lay so close to the river, beneath a stand of sycamores, that most of the women and all the children who stayed aboard the boat could hear and see everything.

"Eben woulda loved this place," Grady told the others. Tom agreed.

"He'll be looking out over the water for every boat that passes now, for all eternity."

Once again on the river, George called everyone not on a keel or at the rudder to a meeting in the big cabin, which had been opened up to the night air. At the gathering, everyone had a steaming cup of stew, served in a cup fashioned from a gourd. As the group ate vegetable stew with boiled chunks of fish caught from the river, George spoke. "I want you all to understand how proud I am of each and every one of you. You've all shown real grit getting this far on this here Freedom Train Boat."

A cheer went up.

George held up his hand to still the crowd. "But...but we still have a long way to go to be truly free."

"We're on the Freedom Trail!" shouted one woman.

"The Uner-ground Railroad for real!" shouted another.

Grady lifted his gourd of soup in a toast, saying, "Eben was right all along. This boat is our ticket to freedom after all. Only wish he was here to see it."

"We won't officially be free until we reach Mr. Fairfield's, and then you may relax some, 'cause he'll see every one of you on to Canada. Until then, we're still not free to just float past Hannibal tomorrow and right on up the Mississippi without someone's going to stop us."

Everyone quieted on hearing this. They knew George was right.

"Chances may be slim," said Tom, "but they be better than we had with the sheriff."

"Are we going to hang for shooting the sheriff?" asked one woman.

Ichabod answered her, saying, "No, but what George says is true. Someone, somewhere, be it in Hannibal or north of there, may want to trade with the massa of this here keelboat. Someone's going to want to board us."

George stood and paced among them. "We've got to put more than our backs into this effort. We gotta use our heads."

Ichabod agreed. "We need a good plan. George and I have talked it over, and we got to take a day to hold up."

Grady and Tom came instantly to their feet, Grady asking, "What're you talking about? Hold up?"

"We got to run north, fast as we can," said Tom.

"Why we need to hold up?" asked Daisy.

"You'll all need the time for sitting and thinking and learning," replied Ichabod.

"Learning what?" asked Grady.

"Learning exactly who you are, Mr. Ezeekiel Radcliff," replied George going straight to Grady and handing him a piece of paper.

"My names Grady, sometimes Guthrie...Grady Guthrie Grimes after my massa's name."

"No," said George, firmly pointing to the paper in his hands, "your name's Radcliff, Ezeekiel Radcliff. Says so on that paper in your hand."

"That's your freedom papers, Mr. Radcliff," added Ichabod, "your ticket on the Underground Railroad."

Grady turned to his friends. "Y'all hear that? I got a new name. Says so right here."

"You still just Grady, Grady," replied Tom. "No piece of paper's going to change that."

147

George waved his hands and shook his head, shouting, "No! He is no longer Grady Grimes, and can't think so, ever again. All of you must help one another to take on new names, new identities and a new way of thinking."

"New way of thinking?" asked Tom.

"You got to think like a free man," said Ichabod.

"You have to climb into the head of this here Ezeekiel Radcliff," George said to Grady, again pointing to the paper in his hand, "and you have to *become* him!"

"You, Tom Grimes," shouted Ichabod, handing him a paper. "You ain't Tom Grimes no more. You're Charles Wileford the Third."

"The Third? I likes that."

Grady smiled wide, held up the paper and shouted, "Ezeekiel Radcliff, that'd be me, born a free man in Ohio, March 11, 1824."

"That makes you twenty-nine years of age," George instructed Grady. George pointed to a line on the paper and added, "This is your mother's name, Mattie Lou Willoughby, and your pappy's name is Thaddeus, both residing freeborn in Ohio."

Grady's face took on a glow of pride. "I got family in Ohio?"

"You do now."

Outside a rainstorm began, and the keelboatmen, on orders given them earlier by George, pulled in to shore and tied to. The sound of the rain increased with flashes of lightning and thunder.

"You got to memorize it all so it come right off your tongue like you growed up with it, son," said Ichabod. "All of you have to take on a new name and history, if you want to make free."

George added, "And along with your new names, you're going to learn how to act free. You can't think yourselves slaves no more; if'n you do, they'll know it from everything you say and do. You have to think like a free man, not a slave and not a runaway."

Grady's face fell, and he said, "We still look like slaves, no matter how we change our names. Anybody can tell from the clothes on our backs."

"You quit thinking yourself a slave, Grady, and your clothes'll pass for just fine. It's not what's on your back, it's what's on your mind counts."

"George and me," began Ichabod, "we been studying on the problem. Got some clothes left by the sheriff and some drapes the ladies can refashion, but we'll be needing some additional. Going to find a way. Meantime, you all get to studying on your new names and family histories. Can't have no slipups if anyone boards us."

"Sounds like a fool plan," muttered Tom, but Sissy stepped up to George and loudly asked, "What's my new name? Where're my papers, so I can get studying 'em right off?"

George pulled forth a paper from his pouch, declaring Sissy, "Miss Mary Eloise Smith."

"Why, what a fine name," said Daisy.

"Mary Eloise Smith," repeated Sissy. "Sounds like... like a queen."

"Got a mighty fine sound to it," agreed Ichabod.

"What's your freeman's name, George?" asked Sissy.

"George Henry Hillock."

Everyone laughed now. "I be the Third," said Tom. "Why, because my pappy had the same name, and his pappy before him."

Ichabod waved a hand and shouted them down, saying, "Now listen here! George can read, I can read some, anyone else here who can read raise your hand, even if it's only a little."

Of the fifty or so people assembled two hands timidly rose.

"All right," said Ichabod, "then we have to work hard to teach the others what their freedom papers say. Rest of you, you have to learn your new names like you wore them your whole life."

"So we sit it out here for the night," said George, "until nightfall tomorrow."

"And until you all learn who you is!" added Daisy.

"Can't never use your slave name even inside your head, ever again," added Ichabod.

George finished with, "Any lawman we run up on, he is going to want to know who you are, now! Not who you once were!"

Suddenly someone from onshore shouted, "Hello on the boat! Can we come aboard? Out of the storm?"

Everyone froze. "My Lord, it's over before it's begun," whispered Daisy.

Everyone looked to George to do something, and when Grady lifted a gun, George held up a firm hand, calmly staring at Grady but talking to Daniel. "Daniel, you're the master of this here keelboat for now, so go out and greet our guests."

"What do I say, George?"

"Just open the door a peek and tell 'em you're all full up, tell 'em you got the smallpox aboard, anything to keep their feet onshore."

"Shelter for the night! We saw your lights!" cried out the man from shore. "Just me and my boys!"

Daniel went shakily to the door and peered out into the gloom. He saw a man in a rain slicker, with several younger men standing around him. Each of them was dressed in a long raincoat. All were white, tall and looked serious.

Daniel whispered back to George, "There's four whites, all with long guns and dogs."

"Runaway catchers," moaned Ichabod.

"Colfax is the name! Isacc Colfax and sons!" shouted the older man.

"Tell them to come on inside, Daniel," ordered George, lowering his weapon and smiling.

"What?"

Grady and Tom glared at George.

"Just allow them inside. Everyone stay calm. I think I know these men," said George.

Daniel shouted over the pounding storm. "You're welcome to come inside for a spell, warm yourself by the fire." He then stepped back and swung the door wide. The men stepped through one at a time, each ducking the overhead beam. As soon as all four were inside, staring at the collection of black people, Grady jabbed a gun into the leader's'cheek and said, "Welcome aboard, you lowlife bounty hunters."

"We can use their clothes," said Tom.

George held his hands up, having put his rifle aside. "Grady, no need for the gun, and Tom, no man here could fill Mr. John Fairfield's shoes, so we won't even try."

"George!" shouted Fairfield. "We come a long piece to find you!"

"This here boat is a fine place for reunionin'," said Daisy, her contagious smile lighting the room.

CHAPER SIXTEEN

PUSHING NORTH TOWARD FREEDOM

Ichabod stepped around George and took Fairfield's hand, pumping it wildly. "We heard tell a lot about you from George."

Daisy stepped closer and hugged Fairfield, introducing herself as George's mother. "I owe you so much, me an my boy," she said softly.

Sissy brought in some steaming stew for the Underground Railroad men. "Y'all just come sit by the fire and dry your clothes," she suggested.

Ichabod and George sat with the Fairfield men before the blazing fire. "Lord works in mysterious ways, mysterious ways," said Ichabod, looking into the flame.

"How'd you find me?" asked George.

"Not sure," said Fairfield, "but my boys and me have been everywhere you've been, George. Got your scent at Colonel Halverston's, went on to Blainys, and since we missed you there, we turned back for the river, on our way back to our boat, but the storm took her, and we just stumbled onto your light."

"Heard tales of a crazy black bounty hunter and his dog, running runaways," said one of Fairfield's sons, and they all laughed. "Where'd you get a half-baked notion like that, George?"

"It seemed a smart idea at the time, and it took me pretty far."

Mr. Fairfield was stern now. "You should've confided in me before running off, George."

"He's always had a problem with that, my boy has," said Daisy.

"So I see," replied Fairfield. "But this stunt, George, jeopardizes all that my boys and I have worked for for years. You know everything about our operation, every station house, every line, every signal, the cargo, freight and packages stopping and going along the way. Someone in law enforcement catches you and beats that kind of information from you, my boys and me will rot in prison somewhere."

"You needn't have worried. I would never tell no one about you, Mr. Fairfield."

"Really? And I suppose all these good people read about me in the *Missouri Democrat?*" He waved a hand to include everyone listening in. "They all knew my name as soon as you pronounced it, George."

"These my family, Mr. Fairfield. Every one of them is sworn to keep your secrets."

"I hope you're right, George."

"Nobody could ever make me tell about you and your road, Mr. John," said Sissy, ladling him more stew. "They'd have to cut my heart out before I'd tell."

"That goes double for me," said Ichabod.

Fairfield and his boys smiled and nodded at the enthusiasm for keeping their secrets, but they were also aware of the more sullen member of the group.

"Well, folks, " began Fairfiled, "I look around me, and I see near fifty people who know what I stand for and precisely who I am. I have to tell you, it's the first time I've ever revealed myself in Missouri an honest man with no disguise. It feels good. I'm glad you all know how important our work is, and that it must remain secret, so long as the laws stand as they are."

"But pa," said one of his sons, "look here what George has accomplished. It takes years of planning to get a group this size out of bondage. Now here we have fifty people who need our help."

"We haven't ever tried to run out more than five or six at a time, at most," added a second son.

"The Mississippi River is the most traveled path in these here United States," said Fairfield. "It'd never work, boys."

George lifted his buckskin pouch. "I made out papers for fifty, Mr. Fairfield. I come first and foremost for my momma, but I knew there'd be more willing to come out."

"Fifty sets of papers? All up to your usual standards, George? You must have been planning this for a year."

"And then some. And as far as giving away your secrets or being a liability to the Underground Railroad, I ain't talked to no white man 'cept for Colonel Halverston."

Fairfield turned on Daniel and asked, "What's he, if he's not white."

Daisy defended Daniel immediately, "He's different."

"We'd all be on the auction block in St. Louis by now if it hadn't been for Daniel," said George.

"He helped in our escape," added Ichabod. "You can trust Daniel."

Grady gruffly said, "That's right. Risked his own white skin for all 'un us."

Grady's men cheered and nodded their agreement.

"St. Louis, huh?" asked Fairfield.

"Auction block, huh?' asked his elder son.

Fairfield's set eyes and square jaw softened now. "How'd you come to get all these people free, Daniel? A whole boatload of former slaves? How many lawmen do you people have after you, George? And why the devil are you sitting up under these trees as such easy targets? Not so I could find you? Why aren't you all pushing for north?"

"North!" shouted Grady, "sounds like a real place to me for first time in my life."

"North," repeated Tom, his eyes glistening with thoughts of freedom.

"North, North," the group began to chant. George jumped on a chair and shouted everyone down. "Not before you all learn your lines!"

That quited everyone down in agreement.

"Storming out over the big muddy anyhow," soothed Ichabod.

Now, George and Ichabod recounted the story from the time Daniel first met George, and they explained their plan to the Fairfields.

All night and half of the next day, the slaves studied their new identities with the four Fairfield men now helping them out with reading and memorization work. By late afternoon, the sky turned black as night and the rain raged again.

The keelboat took advantage of the bad weather and fewer people being on the river. She moved northward.

CHAPTER SEVENTEEN

THE ROAD IS THE WAR

The men took turns at the keels. When the current and the storm made forward movement impossible, they moved closer to shore. Now men were pulling at overhead tree limbs to move the boat along the next foot. At least here, the water wasn't so angry.

George, Fairfield, his oldest son, Ichabod, Grady, Tom, Daisy and Sissy sat worrying over how they meant to get past Hannibal. "Maybe we ought to split into smaller groups," Fairfield was saying, "some taking to ground, others staying afloat."

The idea was met with a chorus of nays. No one wanted to split up. Then Grady said, "If it makes everyone else safer, then me and Tom and some of the boys, we can go our own way."

"No, we run this out together!" George stood, adamant.

"Be reasonable, George. Anyone get a look inside here, see this many black people assembled, what're they going to think?"

"I don't know, maybe they'll think we're all on some excursion."

This made several break into laughter. "Yeah, Charles Wileford the Third is cruisin' the river," said Tom. "What's so strange 'bout that?"

"You Blainy slaves got some good clothes on your backs," said Grady, "but us Grimes men, freedom papers or not, we don't stand a chance. We are still looking like slaves."

"How many sets of clothing do we need here, George?" asked Fairfield.

"Maybe as many as forty."

"If we had the material, we could make 'em," said Sissy.

"Even if we had the material, Sissy, we ain't got the time," Daisy softly corrected her. George squeezed Sissy's hand in his. The two had become sweet on each other.

"It's a kind thought, Sissy," George said to her.

"Sarah, my real name's Sarah," she corrected him.

"No, no it can't be. It's Mary Eloise Smith. Get that firm in your head, Mary Eloise."

Daniel could stand no more of the worrisome problems facing them, so he stepped out on deck to enjoy the storm. As soon as he did, he saw a light in the distance, way out across the river. The light blinked on and off, far to the north, but it appeared to be coming right for them. Several of the keelboatmen on deck were pointing now, some making out the outline of a steamboat. "Steamer!" shouted one.

"Appears to be in trouble!" shouted another.

Daniel ducked back inside and shouted to George and the others, "A steamboat's heading for us! Coming up north way!"

All the men raced outside and stood silently on deck in the storm, watching the approaching light. The steamer's light reflected off the mist and a growing fog, making it appear larger and closer than it was.

"It's a steamer all right," said George.

Mr. Fairfield asked his eldest son, Robert, to have a look. The young man climbed onto the roof of the flatboat and stared out over the water. "She's a beaut, pa, a side paddle-wheeler! Heading right for us, but she's half-sunk! Must've hit a bad spot in the storm and got heaved to. She may be underwater by time she reaches us."

"Seeing anyone on board?" asked Fairfield.

"No, pa, she look's deserted."

"Keep your eyes on her son." Turning to Ichabod, Fairfield said, "You must've done some powerful praying, Mr. Ichabod. If that's a downed steamer, there'll be leftover trunks and bags filled with clothing on board."

George stared at Fairfield. "Tom, Grady and me, we'll go."

"Boarding a moving steamboat caught in the current can be tricky, George, and if you're going to get in and out with enough to make it worth your while, you'll need plenty of hands. Six, maybe seven at least," replied Fairfield.

"I won't endanger your sons, Mr. Fairfield, not any more than I already have."

The younger son, Jason, perhaps twenty, stepped up to his father and George. He said firmly, "I'm old enough to make my own decisions, and I'm going aboard her."

The eldest son, Robert, hopped down from the roof and said, "She's completely abandoned, pa, but water's dragging her down fast. Count me in."

His third son, William, volunteered as well, and Fairfield said, "My sons speak for themselves."

Daniel stepped up to the men and pointed to a small rowboat tied to the back of the flatboat "I can handle the oars on that boat if Grady and Tom will get it into the water."

Grady and Tom got the boat into the water, and Fairfiled placed his hand on Daniel's shoulder, asking, "Think you can keep the boat in tight, son? The water's mean and choppy, and the steamer'll be beating you off. It'll be a wild ride."

"I can do it. I've had lots of experience holding a boat."

"We've got plenty of men can handle the boat," said George, not wanting to place Daniel in such danger.

"None of them can swim. Leastways George, if I fall over the side, I got a chance."

Ichabod said, "George, the boy's right. They still don't give slaves swimming lessons."

George nodded slowly and agreed to Daniel's piloting the boat.

Daniel looked up again to see that the steamer, closer now, looked like a floating palace, as if Colonel Halverston's mansion had been thrown into the river. But it listed to one side.

"Men," said Fairfield, "we have to be careful out there, and keep it simple. Get on, find any trunks you can and get off. You won't have but a blink of time before that old girl is under the Mississippi."

Everyone going climbed down off the keelboat and into the rowboat. Daniel took one oar, Robert Fairfield took the other, for the time being.

The rain came down in slanting, stinging pellets. The river swelled over the sides of the little boat, and the water was cold as it filled the boat to their ankles.

The light of the crippled steamboat coming at them over the black river proved fearsome. Boarding a steamer in mid-river, one in control and operating, was difficult and risky even by daylight. Boarding one out of control and only half above water from a small craft could be disasterous.

George shouted over the storm, "Pull that'a way!"

Daniel fought the left oar and Robert the right. Their rowing proved accurate, strong and trained, and they fell into sync with one another. The fear in the others calmed as they watched Daniel and Robert cut a clean course right for the steamer. Whenever the boat twirled around with the powerful current, Daniel expertly worked his oar or Robert worked his to right it. If the spin was too strong, they lifted both oars clear out of the water, allowed the river its way with the boat, and after the boat righted itself, they continued.

"Where'd you learn how to handle an oar like that?" asked George of Daniel.

"Whenever I could," Daniel began as he rowed, "I'd get me down to the wharf at Hannibal. There was an old feller there who hired out boats for people to go across the river. He paid me to take folks out, and once or twice I got caught up in bad weather. Don't take a strong man, just a good notion about right and left, and how oars best work in the water. I admit, my arms are tuckered out some!"

"How we going to board that steamer?" asked Grady.

The steamboat loomed up large behind Daniel now, and looking over his shoulder, he watched the lights grow sharper. He could see the huge smoke stack and side-wheel. The poor listing ship looked like a wounded white whale.

Tom and the others were bailing water from the bottom of the rowboat. George studied the steamboat from all angles as he would any problem. Finally, he said, "The wheel, Daniel! Head for the paddle-wheel. There's a ladder alongside it, and it'll place us dead center of the steamboat when we board. We can fan out from there."

As the steamer came near, Daniel and Robert rowed in easier. Grady stood now at the prow of their small boat and almost fell overboard, but he righted himself and let fly the rope like a cowboy. The rope missed its target, but a second attempt caught hold. The men cheered.

For a moment, they felt the steamboat's pull, but Grady held firm to the rope, and he and the others began to tug and pull the small boat tight into the monster steamboat's paddle-wheel. They came to rest at the ladder.

"Can you see her letters?" asked Daniel.

"W-A-L-T-E-R," read young Robert Fairfield aloud as Grady tied off the rope.

"Why, she's the *Walter Scott,*" said Daniel, sad at having learned the fate of the gilded, proud steamer.

"You know of her?" asked George.

"She put in at Hannibal all the time," he replied. "She was a beauty, she was. So proud and piping with organ music all the time. Playing "Dixie" all the time real loud whenever she made her way into Hannibal. She was getting old, her paint peeling about the edges, and her black iron rusting, but she was big."

"Did she carry slave cargo?" asked George.

Daniel reluctantly nodded, "Many times. Not always, but many. They'd be out on the deck at the stern, there with the wood piles, the bails of cotton and the flax. I didn't never think of them much. None of the boys did. We'd all grown up with the sight."

"See what's come of your proud, old steamer?" George said. "Same thing's going to come of the whole state of Missouri and the South—when war comes over slavery, Daniel. Free states and slaves states are heading toward a collision, and its going to bring half this nation to its knees. And it'll all come because of those black folks riding up and down this river on boats like the *Walter Scott,* treated like so much cattle or wheat or cotton, those black people nobody in Missouri thinks about now."

"You really think there's a war coming over slavery?"

"Yeah. A war between the states."

Daniel gave it thought for some moments, asking, "When'll it come?"

"A year, maybe two, maybe ten."

"What does Mr. Fairfield say about it?"

"He thinks it'll come in less than ten years, and he says there ain't nothing anyone can do now to stop it. All the talk in Washington, all the law-making against slavery, it's all led straight for war, he says. It's why the Underground Railroad is so busy these days."

"White men and black, who can't sit by any longer and watch slavery go on in this country, are taking action," said Robert Fairfield in Daniel's ear. "In some ways, the war's already started. The Road is the war."

"Robert, his brothers and his father, me, too, I reckon," began George, "we're the first soldiers along with thousands like us."

"I guess then that I'm a soldier, too," said Daniel.

The boat bumped against the steamer, hugged her and was tied tightly now. The men started up the ladder and along the side-wheel with Grady and Tom in the lead. Robert and his brothers followed, and then George left, shaking Daniel's hand as if for the last time. Each man made the difficult climb up to the deck.

Daniel, waiting in the boat, tried to get his bearings. *Exactly where are we in relation to the keelboat lights?* Mr. Fairfield had said they would hold the flatboat close to shore on a northerly tact, but as Daniel searched for their light in the dark, he could not find it. Now the feeling of being carried swiftly along by the steamboat wreck began to take hold of him. *Being tied to the side of a great whale could not be so different,* he thought.

Daniel didn't know that Fairfield and the others on the flatboat were this moment watching the steamboat slip rapidly past them, going at a quickening pace toward a dangerous bend. Daniel couldn't know that some of the keelboatmen had already started saying that the speeding steamer would come to a grinding halt amid sandbars, snags, and overhanging willows at the place where Eben Grimes had been buried. Everyone feared the steamer would explode. Word spread around the keelboat that Daniel and the men who had followed George would not be returning.

CHAPER EIGHTEEN

FROM EXPLOSION TO EXCURSION

Daniel watched the water level rise over the lettering alongside the steamboat. He realized that the river meant to sink the steamer in quick fashion. He had given up trying to determine where in all the gloom and rain lay the keelboat. He imagined the steamer with him lashed to it had somehow turned completely in the water and the keelboat must be on the other side, out of his view. Now Daniel worried about George and the other men aboard the steamboat, as the water mark along her side indicated she'd dropped three feet since they'd attached. The *Walter Scott* could capsize any time now.

Then Daniel saw the river bend coming at them. It appeared some three or four hundred yards off, but it loomed large and mean-looking. The steamer and everyone on it would be dashed against the bend. Daniel started up the ladder to warn the others, but suddenly the steamer lurched and Daniel was thrown into the water. Daniel felt the strong pull of the current at his feet. Somehow he'd grabbed hold of the rowboat and held on for life. Overhead, he heard George shout, "Stay in the boat!"

He looked up to see Grady, Tom, George and the Fairfield sons, their arms loaded with suitcases, trunks and loose clothing, all trying to manage a foothold on the ladder. Between them, Grady and Tom held onto a huge steamer trunk.

"You can't put that on the boat!" shouted George to them. "It's too much weight in this storm. It'll sink us sure."

Robert Fairfield solved the problem with a gunshot to the lock, and in a moment clothes were raining down on Daniel where he had climbed back into the boat. Tom and Grady insisted on emptying the contents with no regard for what floated down into the water and what hit the boat. Meanwhile, the Fairfield boys and George had made it back into the small boat, and Daniel pointed out both the bend ahead which threatened to kill them all, and the fact he had lost sight of the keelboat.

"How're we going to find our way back, George?" asked Daniel.

"I saw the keelboat light from the deck," said Tom as he made the leap from ladder to boat. The climb down was much easier since the water level had risen so high up the ladder. "They're north of us! We went whizzing right on by them."

The steamboat lurched again, pulling the small boat out of the water. George and Tom worked to cut the lines. Daniel shouted, "What about Grady? He's still up there!"

With the ropes cut, the small boat crashed back into the river and slipped away from the steamer. Grady fell onto the side-wheel and refused to jump from it.

"Jump, man, its your only chance," yelled Tom.

"Jump!" chanted the others.

"I can't swim!" he shouted back.

"So, you goin' to die up there or down here with your friends?" shouted Tom.

"I'll ride her out till she hits a snag or land!" he bawled back.

Just then, the *Walter Scott* came forward at them, keeling over as if to smash them all, and Grady lost his hold. Thrown into the raging river, he came up screaming. Without hesitation, Daniel tied a rope around himself and dove in to help Grady.

"Throw out some ropes!" shouted George to the others. "Fool boy's going to get himself killed!"

Daniel swallowed water and spit a lot out, while he called Grady's name and swam for the spot where he had last surfaced. He heard Grady before he saw him. The big man shouted, "Help! I'm here!"

"Mr. Grady, take hold of the rope around my waist and hold firm," Daniel said. "The rope's attached to the boat. It's our lifeline, Mr. Grady. Hold on."

The big man was frantic with fear, but he focused on Daniel's words and did as told. Another rope hit Grady across the face, and he grabbed onto it. "They done lassoed me!" he yelled.

Daniel and Grady felt themselves being tugged toward the rowboat, now well away from the sinking steamer. As Daniel and Grady fell into the wet bottom of the rowboat, the steamboat hit the sandbar at the river's bend, not fifty yards from where they'd bobbed and twirled cork-like in the water. The black sky was suddenly alight with the grandest and most awful fireball Daniel had ever seen.

"Looks like the *Walter Scott*'s run right into something too big for it to move," George said quietly.

⧗ ⧗ ⧗

Daisy sat crying alongside an equally tearful Sissy. Others in the big cabin on the flatboat cried as well, and Mr. Fairfield sadly contemplated the loss of his sons.

Daisy said, "Not fair! Just ain't fair to find my boy, George, only to lose him like this. And that poor sweet boy, Daniel Webster Jackson."

"Why'd we let them go off and do such a fool thing?" asked Sissy. "Blown to smithereens, every one of 'em."

"Burn't to a sizzling crisp," someone was in the midst of saying when Daniel, followed by the others, sauntered into the cabin, each swinging clothing and bags.

George shouted, "We didn't have time to take sizes, but we got our arms loaded. You all just step up and find what fits you."

Daniel thought, *While the clothes are soaking wet, these howls of happiness and pleasure are warm enough to dry them out.*

"George!" shouted Daisy, hugging him, and then grabbing Daniel and doing likewise. "You're all safe!"

"All present and accounted for, pa," said Robert to his father who hugged each of his sons.

"We gave you all up for dead when we saw the explosion," said Fairfield.

Grady, still shaken from his ordeal in the water, found himself surrounded by well-wishers, and Tom strutted about as a hero, holding clothes over his head, saying, "Our shopping trip went mighty fine!"

Grady told the others about Daniel's bravery. Everyone wanted the entire story, and as the heroes were warmed with hugs and mugs of coffee and stew, everybody listened to the adventure. As the story unfolded, so did the clothing, as each person on the keelboat located something he or she liked.

"Here you are Mr. Wileford," said one woman to Tom. "This vest would look right smart on you."

"Something here for you, too, Mr. Radcliff, Sissy said to Grady, holding up a pair of suspenders."

Another lady said to Sissy, "Why Miss Smith, mayn't this be your bonnet?" Sissy took the hat and tried it on for size, George helping her with the blue lace about her chin.

"Why, look at this scarlet scarf!" said Daisy. "I won't wear scarlet. Ain't never going to be *that* free!"

"Mr. Palmer," suggested Robert Fairfield, addressing Ichabod in his freeman's name, "I bet these green pants are about your size, and they'd go fine with a white shirt."

Daisy disappeared for a while and reappeared in the doorway completely changed. She wore an emerald green dress with fluffy feathers all around the collar, and a sash of yellow about her waist. Obviously a large woman had once owned the dress, but Daisy looked as if she could hardly breathe in it. She wore yellow gloves up to her elbows, and a huge green feathered hat made her look like a rooster. She struggled to walk in a pair of yellow shoes she'd worked onto her feet.

Ichabod looked on in amazement. Daisy said to him, "Well, what's the matter with you, old man? Ain't you never seen a lady before?"

"Oh, Daisy," he said, his eyes wide, "you're...you're beautiful."

Throwing back her head and almost falling in her new shoes, she laughed. Ichabod grabbed her by the waist to help right her. Then he backed away as if she might break. He repeated, "You just looks so beautiful, Daisy."

George agreed, adding, "You sure do, momma."

"You just every one of you remember this! I'm the widow Mrs. George Henry Hillock on travel excursion with my only-est son, George. I'm a freeborn black woman on holiday. Come to visit. Paid my fare to Mr. Colfax," she said, pointing to Mr. Fairfield. "The operator of this here excursion boat."

Everyone laughed and each began to talk in the same manner. John Fairfield had told them that with the clothes they'd found, they could set up an elaborate scheme. Mr. Fairfield was to be called Mr. Isaac Colfax, the owner and operator of the Sights and Wonders of the Mississippi River Excursion Company. George had been busy at work, making out a bill of sale on the boat in the name of Isaac Colfax and Sons, and a formal listing about the company, costs, and schedule. Most of the people would pose as passengers, like Daisy, freeborn black people, with their freedom papers and their newfound wardrobes. The plan stood a fair chance, and by now all of the "free" men and women aboard had learned their lessons about their identities and histories.

Mr. Fairfield joked, "Who'd believe anyone was stupid enough or brave enough to attempt running off with fifty slaves right up the river in full daylight?" But as he said it, he cocked his head first to one side, and then the other, deep in thought. He shouted, "By George! Who'd believe anyone that crazy?"

George knew this meant something special. He approached Fairfield and said, "You're hatching a new plan. What is it?"

Fairfield frowned and shook his head to indicate no, and said, "It's too risky."

Ichabod asked, "What's too risky?"

"We stick with the Colfax Excursion plan, but we take it one bold step further."

"Meaning?" asked Daisy, joining in the pow-wow.

"Meaning, my lady, we brazen it out boldly."

"So, we begin by putting up a big sign over the top of the boat?" asked George. "A sign reading out The Colfax Excursion Line?"

"That's a fine start," replied Fairfield. "Do you think we could get up a sign?"

"All we need is to locate some paint aboard."

"There's some canvas aboard," added Daniel, warming to the idea.

"But what's this brazen plan?" asked Ichabod of Fairfield.

"Don't you know?"

Ichabod's eyes lit up and he shouted, "We go straight into Hannibal under our own steam! Just like that."

"I get it," added Daniel. "We're supposed to stop there as one of the wonderments of the Mississippi. After all, it is a real wilderness town. No self-respecting river excursion tour would miss it."

"Right!" said Mr. Fairfield. "We'll have George add it to the schedule."

Everyone looked about at one another, some grumbling. "Do you think we can get away with that, George?" asked Daisy. "I mean, it is risky."

"There's no way we can slip by Hannibal without being seen, even at night," replied George. "Before they stop us and make us come into the landing at Hannibal, we'll come in on our own. Brazen it out, like Mr. Fairfield says."

"Colfax, George," he corrected. "Best everybody begins now calling me and my boys by Colfax."

George held up his hand, saying, "There's people in Hannibal who will recognize Daniel, and the judge there knows me as George Penny, the runaway catcher."

Daniel waved him down, saying, "I plum forgot to tell you that Judge Hatcher ain't judge of Hannibal no more."

"What?"

"According to Sheriff Brisbane, Judge Halverston's come to office."

"Spying agrees with you, Daniel. That's mighty fine information, and it could be a great help getting past our problems with Hannibal."

"Who's this Halverston?" asked Fairfield.

"A good friend. Got his own road operation near Hannibal."

Daniel told Fairfield about the colonel, Old Billy and how they worked their station on the Underground Railroad.

"Maybe our luck's changing, folks," said George.

CHAPTER NINETEEN

A TRULY BRAZEN ACT

The old, gray flatboat, once the most drab thing afloat, was now decked out on each side with big signs proclaiming the boat to be Isaac Colfax's Mississippi River Excursion Boat. The lettering was beautiful, going from two-feet in size to regular lettering on the list of places visited by the Colfax Excursion Line. Large rippling red ribbons flowed from stem to stern, these created by Sissy from discarded clothes and scarves. All along the deck of the flatboat, couples strolled arm-in-arm, Daisy with Ichabod, George with Sissy, Tom and Grady with their partners. Fourteen of the men were working the poles and rudder, and they had easy parts to play, as they didn't have to pretend to be anyone but themselves, acting as slaves to Mr. Isaac. George had made out a bill of sale on each of these men, and Colfax's name figured in the ownership papers. These men worked the keels and lifted and toted boxes in shifts. Colfax's sons pretended to be mean to these men, shouting orders and threats. Meanwhile, Daniel had officially become the galley boy to help out with the cooking.

As they neared the landing at Hannibal, Mr. Fairfield cautioned everyone. "You're on your own now. Hold tight to your freedom papers, whatever happens. Even if we're arrested, we have proof we are who we say we are."

"Don't show your papers to anybody but the judge," George instructed them. "Show them to the wrong man, and he'll just eat 'em raw."

Daisy twirled a big white parasol. Overhead, lacey trim flew at its edges as she walked alongside Ichabod. Ichabod muttered to Daisy, "I hope we made the right decision."

"Don't worry. George and Mr. Fairfield know what they're doing."

"This is going to be something, if it works," replied Sissy as she and George strolled by.

Hearing this, Mr. Fairfield shouted, "Brazen it out, Mary Eloise, Mrs. Hillock!"

"What about you, Mr. Radcliff?" George asked of Tom. "You doing all right?"

Tom lifted his cane and twirled it between his fingers. Smiling, he said, "I bet they ain't never seen a bunch like us before. The name of Ezeekiel Radcliff will long be remembered in these parts!" The cane snapped back into place at Tom's heel.

People around them laughed at Tom's show of sass, and Mr. Fairfield said, "That's it folks! We're on a riverboat excursion, and people laugh and have fun on holiday, so laugh it up! We want folks yonder at the wharf in Hannibal to be downright jealous. Pass the word! Whoop it up. No sourpusses and no fear!"

George agreed, saying, "We're also sight-seers, so I want everyone looking and gawking and straining to see, and you're to make opinions on what you see." He then asked Daniel to help spread the word.

Hannibal had come into sight, and now a crowd began to form at the landing, everyone curious about the strangely decked-out flatboat with the big sign atop it. As they neared the landing, they saw some boys waving hats and some grownups shouting a welcome. This excitement was soon replaced by a curious agitation as the boat drew nearer and everyone saw the color of the passengers' skin. The crowd that had gathered began to swell, yet as it did so, it became quieter, the people talking among themselves, the hat-waving finished. Daniel saw boys sent off, possibly to alert authorities. Others returned with friends and relatives to see the amazing Colfax Excursion Boat.

"We're committed now!" shouted Fairfield. "Looks like some official-looking types are coming out to greet us, boys, George!"

Looking finer and prouder than she had any right to look, the aged flatboat moved in as the black people aboard continued their charade, laughing and strolling the deck, some waving now to the people on shore, Daisy twirling her parasol, Tom his cane. The smiles and laughter coming from the excursioning people kept the crowd on the wharf wondering. Suddenly, the clatter of a base drum, a fiddle, a horn and a flute erupted, and Hannibal's four-piece band began marching down Hannibal's main street and to the landing, the crowd parting to allow them through.

"Judge Halverston's got a hand in this, I warrant," said Daniel to George and Mr. Fairfield.

"What a fine welcome Hannibal wants for us, folks!" shouted Fairfield over the noise, and Daniel could feel everyone's confidence onboard rise with each new selection of the band. After playing "Dixie," the band went to "Turkey in the Straw."

With the boat secured, Mr. Fairfield went into his act as Isaac Colfax by leaping onto the cabin roof and standing by the banner which proclaimed his name and his business in two-foot high lettering. The crowd fell instantly silent, anxious to hear the showman talk. Isaac Colfax wore a black suit, vest and top hat, and his beard and mustache lent a respectable air, and he looked like a ringmaster in a circus. "Ladies and Gentlemen, boys and girls of Hannibal!" he began. "The Colfax Excursion Tour of the Great Mississippi has not received so warm and hospitable a welcome in all of its ports-of-call as this! Not in New Orleans and not in Vicksburg or St. Louis!"

The crowd cheered at this.

"Friends, friends and citizens of Hannibal! We have traveled the river from its beginnings in Minnesota to its terminus at the Gulf of Mexico and back, my friends, and we have not met warmer, kinder souls on our journey than yours right here in Hannibal, Missouri!"

Again the crowd cheered and hats flew up over-head.

Mr. Fairfield told them who he was, introduced his sons, his crew, including Daniel, and with a wave of the hand, he indicated his passengers. "Fine upstanding black citizenry of the free states of the North, free men, women and children who had been smitten with the curiosity of their race to see how people in the South really live...and how you all really treat your slaves. These folks don't want to hear it from the newspapers, dime novels or abolitionist preachers, my friends. No, they come to visit in order to see the wonders of the South firsthand."

This is truly a brazen act, Daniel thought.

Colfax, continued, "My father and his father before him led excursions up and down every river system in this here country, and I took up the slack! Born of an adventurer, I have myself become one, and I expect my sons will carry on with the Colfax Excursion Line when I am gone on to my reward! But today is not a day for speaking of the grim or grand prospects that lie ahead, my friends. No today is a day to speak of the price of a ticket aboard the Colfax Excursion Tour. We are, admittedly, on the last leg of our arduous voyage, but we do have a number of berths left aboard for any man bold enough, and with enough coin jingling in his pocket, to take you onboard!"

"What's left to see on your tour?" shouted a black man in the crowd on the wharf, and Daniel saw that it was Old Billy. "Can't be much left if'n you're going north from here."

"Why, you'll travel to the most exotic cities along the river north of Missouri! Into the great northern reaches, to see Keokuk, Clinton, Dubuque, Moline, Rock Island and Freeport."

"What about St. Paul and Minnesota?" asked Judge Halverston.

"Where's that?" asked another in the crowd.

"On the schedule!" replied Colfax to both questions with a resounding thud of the cane he had been clutching and punctuating his words with.

"Up the river, boys!" shouted Robert Fairfield to bolster his father's efforts.

"Why Hannibal's my latest addition to the schedule, folks! And I can pick you up here now and have you back before Christmas dinner. All a man needs is the four-dollar fee and the good sense to use it wisely."

As the crowd cheered this, Mr. Colfax's slaves acted the part of slaves, resting from their labors, while Colfax's paying customers, the black sight-seers, made a great show of curiosity about Hannibal and its people. They stared and pointed out such things as the clock tower, the church steeple and the grocery to one another. Daisy had flipped out a pair of glases on a stick and she placed them up to her eyes, working hard to see something Ichabod pointed out, slaves sleeping out on the stern of a steamboat docked alongside them. This human cargo was being carried South. Some of the slaves aboard the steamer had been roused by the noise of the crowd and Colfax's speech-making. One of them began playing a mouth organ, and he fit his sound right in with that of the band on shore.

Colonel Halverston stepped forward and took the gangplank for Colfax's excursion boat. Waving his white hat as he did so, he quieting the crowd. His eyes locked on George and he muttered, "Are you people plain crazy?" But aloud, he shouted, "Folks, folks, everyone!" He gained their attention even as he shook hands with Isaac Colfax. "Unhappy as I am to do this, unfortunate as it is, I cannot allow Mr. Colfax's Excursion Line to operate here."

"What?" burst out one man in the crowd.

"Why not?" asked Colfax, his face wrinkled up in confusion for the benefit of the crowd.

"Because there is no record in the courthouse of any license or payment for use of the landing by his company. And since Mr. Colfax here does not have his papers in order..."

"Oh, come on, judge!" shouted one man in the crowd whom Daniel recognized as the store clerk, eager for the business the sight-seers would bring his way, "Can't that kind of thing be taken care of here and now?"

"Colfax here hasn't got a permit, and he knows how these things work! You have to have your papers in order if you're turning a profit on our landing, sir."

"They'll be needing supplies, judge," countered the store clerk, and meantime, you and Mr. Colfax can work out any details necessary. "We want everyone happy, so that Mr. Colfax will come again with his excursion to Hannibal and not bypass us!"

"You're standing in the way of progress, judge," came another unhappy merchant.

"Progress and trade," said another.

"And hospitality," said a woman in the crowd.

"Why, this could become a regular stopping place for all the showboats, and not just freighters," said another man.

Reverend Thornbush pushed forward, saying, "This here Mr. Colfax and his excursion line means prosperity, perhaps more jobs, Judge Halverston. Why, he's already hired young Daniel Webster Jackson."

"Hip-hip, hurray for Daniel!" shouted Joe Grier, who stood amid the crowd with other town boys, and the others took up the cheer, all beaming with pride to know someone their age with so fine a profession as galley boy on an excursion line. Daniel waved at the crowd.

"He's already got Hannibal on the schedule, judge, dear," moaned Amanda Halverston, the colonel's wife.

"Best do as the missus says, judge," said Old Billy, holding back a laugh.

Fairfield whispered in Halverston's ear, "Nice try, but it looks like we got public opinion on our side."

Both men were shaking hands and smiling at the crowd, but through clenched teeth, Halverston warned, "The longer you stay in Hannibal, the surer someone will discover your secrets, Mr. Fairfield."

Fairfield looked from Halverston to George, realizing how easily this stranger to him had put it all together. Given George's presence, along with Daniel's, it was an easy connection to make.

"Shall I take our passengers on the tour of the town, Pa?" asked Robert Fairfield.

Halverston bit his lip and declared for the crowd, saying, "All right! I know when I'm out-numbered, folks, and I do want your vote come next election. Guess Mr. Colfax and I can strike a deal down at the courthouse."

The passengers of the Colfax Excursion Line and the Hannibal people all erupted into cheers, and Daisy, with Ichabod on her arm, was the first to follow Robert down the gangplank and onto the dusty sand roads of Hannibal. There, Robert, acting as tour guide, led the freeborn black passengers from home to home, taking his cue from a map drawn him by Daniel, pointing out the oldest building in

Hannibal, naming her first pioneers, giving some history, all information Daniel had learned from Mrs. Shorr's schoolroom. They went from public buildings to stores and the livery stable, examining everything.

The passengers in their gay colors of orange, green, yellow, red and blue tipped their hats and smiled at everyone they passed. A crowd of Hannibal people had, from the start of the tour, gathered behind the sight-seers, all curious and interested to know what it was about Hannibal that Robert, the tour guide, had to say.

"When do we gets to see the jail?" asked Grady boldly.

"Always wanted to look in on a real western lawless town jail," said Tom.

"Yeah, where you all keep the outlaws?" asked Sissy with George on her arm.

"You saw some in St. Louis, Miss Eloise," said George. "How come you want to see more of the same?"

Tom twirled his cane and Daisy her parasol, and even from the boat where Daniel had remained behind, he took pride in their boldness and the liveliness in their steps. They'd done it. They had fooled Hannibal into believing the unbelievable, thanks to Mr. Fairfield and everyone's sticking to the plan.

⌛ ⌛ ⌛

Ichabod, Daisy, Sissy, and George, along with most of the passengers who'd stepped down the gangplank and into the life of Hannibal, continued to follow Robert Fairfield's lead, all looking fine in their frilly white shirts, ties and coats, wide-skirted dresses and scarves. They had marched clear to the mill near the south end of town. It was a great grist mill, three stories high, situated on a rock-solid foundation. The huge waterwheel caught the spillover of the Mississippi in a backwash and turned it to good use. The mill ground corn, barley, wheat and oats for surrounding farmers. Robert Fairfield knew well enough to flatter the operator, shake hands and ask him to explain how his mill worked. The owner beamed and explained in glowing terms how his operation kept Hannibal on the map.

Daniel had broken free of the boys at the landing who wanted to hear all about his running away only to come back so fine and heroic with a job on the big excursion boat. He wanted to join the tour, and as he approached the mill, he saw two riders coming at them from the south road, and he recognized Sheriff Brisbane. George and Robert saw him coming, too, and suddenly, the tour was over, everyone hearing Robert say, "Next stop is aways up-river, folks. Time to get ourselves back aboard the *Colfax*. "We're behind schedule, folks!" He tried to keep his voice calm.

"Isn't that Sheriff Brisbane?" asked the mill operator, as he looked down the road.

But George and Robert were no longer at his side and had already herded the group back toward the landing, almost at a run. Trying to keep up a good appearance at the same time, young Robert pointed out the school. Daniel saw a stern Mrs. Shorr giving him the evil-eye. Next Robert pointed out the richest looking houses in Hannibal and the great lighthouse on Cardiff Hill. They passed the smithy shop, the tanner's, the dyer's, sheep pens, pig pens, and the local saloon, Robert commenting on each in fast fashion while keeping everyone moving toward the boat.

People who had known Daniel his entire life, for the first time ever wanted to shake his hand, but he couldn't dawdle. One man said for all to hear, "I never knowed no son of Hannibal who'd become such an important person!" Daniel turned to see it was Reverend Thornbush, beaming and speaking to a group at the livery stable. "Real fashionable all around," commented one of his listeners. Daniel saw the jealous looks darting to him from the boys in Joe Grier's camp.

Joe stepped up and stopped Daniel at the gangplank, and while everyone else was boarding, Joe said, "Wish I'd have gone with you the night you lit out, Daniel. Maybe now I'd be working for the Colfax Line, too. You think you might put in a word for me?"

"I'll do what I can. No promises."

Daniel saw Brisbane and Lem, barreling toward the landing, heading straight for them, but the curious crowd got in their way, one man grabbing the reins of the sheriff's horse, asking what had happened. Brisbane's leg was in bandages, and he looked as if he'd been in a drunken brawl. Lem pointed at Daniel and shouted, "It's them, sheriff! The ones who shot you down!"

George grabbed Daniel by the shoulders. "Mr. Colfax has lifted anchor, son! You going or staying?"

They rushed up the gangplank, leaving the onlookers wondering what was happening. The flatboat moved from the landing, keelmen fast at work as the passengers waved

Hannibal goodbye. Daniel shouted his final goodbye to Joe, and waved his straw hat.

A shot rang out; the bullet whizzed through Daniel's straw hat, and Daniel heard George half shout, half curse as he hit the deck. Sissy screamed. Daniel saw that the sheriff still had his rifle aimed at the boat.

George's blood colored the gray wood deck, his white shirt stained just as quickly. "He's bleeding bad!" shouted Daniel.

Daisy fell to her knees over George, shielding him, crying over his pain and crying for help.

Daniel turned back toward the deck and saw Colonel Halverston knocking Lem off his feet and snatching the rifle from Sheriff Brisbane, calling for men to help him take the shooters into custody.

Mr. Fairfield studied George's wound. "It's bad, folks," he said. We need to get George to a doctor, and that means we have to turn back to Hannibal, now!"

Grady and Tom stood over Fairfield. Grady slowly said, "We ain't turning this boat back for Hannibal and slavery." He held a gun on Mr. Fairfield.

"Are you crazed, man? They'll cut us out of the water at Cardiff Hill!" Mr. Fairfield yelled.

"They'll sell us South for sure if we go back!" Grady shouted.

"If they don't see us turn around now, they'll know we're guilty of making fools of them all, and every man onshore will get a rifle and come to the turkey shoot, Mr. Grady, and my sons and I don't want to become turkeys anymore than you or these other people do! Now do as I say."

Robert Fairfield held a cocked gun to Grady's temple now, saying, "Do as my pa says Mr. Grady, or you won't never have to worry about being sold nowhere ever again in this life."

Grady's jaw worked for a moment. No one breathed. John Fairfield held out a hand to take Grady's gun from him, saying, "This way, no one else gets killed either here or onshore, Mr. Grady."

Grady gave up the gun, but said, "All the same, I'll be making my own way from here; me and Tom have our own plan."

Tom added, "We'll take our chances with the river. Dive in over the lee side."

"No!" shouted Ichabod. "We come into this thing all together, and we'll see it through together. We can still brazen this thing through."

"We try to run," said Fairfield, "and they'll be picking us off from upriver on that bluff. It'll be a blood bath. You want that?'

"How many for letting George's life bleed away?" asked Ichabod. "How many for making free over his death?"

No one stirred. "We still have right on our side," said Daniel. "We're still an excursion company, and you all still have your freedom papers and your freedom attitudes. We go back into Hannibal, and we brazen it out just like we did all morning, only this time, one of us has been unlawful shot by a man who ain't sheriff in these parts no more. We still got colonel and Judge Halverston on our side."

"Daniel's right, we have a good chance to pull this off," said Fairfield.

"Then what're we waiting for?" asked Grady.

"Mr. Wileford," said Tom to Grady, "I believe you're right to be angry over this outrage."

"Indeed, Mr. Radcliff the Third, I am."

"Turn her back for shore, men!" shouted Fairfield, while Robert and Sissy tended to George's wound. "And pass the word. We have our papers, we have rights as American citizens. We'll demand to know why one of my passengers has been shot by this man, Brisbane."

"Dern near got Daniel, too," said Tom, lifting Daniel's hat to show off the hole in it. "Lucky you weren't wearing it."

⌛ ⌛ ⌛

Entering Hannibal Landing for the second time, they found the mood of the crowd grim. The women and children and band had disappeared. Joe Grier and his friends hung back behind barrels. Colfax's passengers and crew faced guns all around. A lone slave aboard the steamer played his mouth organ. All the other slaves at the stern of the paddle-wheeler watched the unfolding drama with great interest. Daniel studied the faces confronting them, searching for Colonel Halverston, and when he did see him, the colonel, too, held a pointed gun, and he was giving the order to fire if anyone showed any sign of resistance. Daniel's heart sank, but he stood tall beside Mr. Fairfield. Mr. Fairfield held out his papers, proof of ownership of the barge, proof of the company's history and habits, proof of his and his son's identities. This set the example for the runaways in his care. Ichabod held up his freedom papers, and the wind rippled them in the breeze. This done, the other slaves lifted out their papers, too.

Colfax leapt onto a crate and then onto the cabin roof again, making of himself an easy target for the sixty or so guns leveled at him, and he shouted, "Gentlemen! I demand to know why? Why has one of your number bloodied my excursion boat? Why have you done this awful deed? I will, sirs, protect the life of every single passenger aboard with my own life's blood." He lifted two huge six-shooters from the holsters about his hips and finished with, "One more volley at the *Colfax,* sirs, and I'll kill every man jack of you, before I am put to my grave!"

Missourians understood bravery when they saw it. Daniel watched as the guns on shore leveled out, Colonel Halverston shouting, "Allow Colfax and his people to give themselves up. If there is any truth to what Mr. Brisbane and his man asserts, then we will get at it in a court of law, and not here on the street. Give these people safe passage to my courthouse," he ordered the new sheriff and his men. "We'll sort this out there! Are you agreeable, Mr. Colfax?"

Colfax took a long moment to scan conditions both on the boat and on the landing. Finally, he said, "We are agreeable sir, and we take your word as that of a man of honor." He lowered his two hog-gutters, and Daniel breathed easier. He had half feared that Colfax might just unload his weapons on the crowd, he was that convincing.

Sheriff Brisbane, held by two men, pointed and shouted, "These men stole my keelboat and all the property I had on it! This here excursion business is a lie!"

"You're no longer sheriff of Hannibal, Mr. Brisbane," shouted the former judge of Hannibal, Judge Hatcher, stepping into the fray. "Since your secretive business ventures often took you away, you were voted out, as was I. When you fired on these freeborn black people, you did so as a private citizen, and not as a representative of the law in Hannibal." He then addressed Colfax, saying, "I for one, sir, am sorely grieved by all this. Was anyone hurt onboard?"

"Yes, Mr. George Hillock, and we desperately need a doctor for him!"

A well dressed man beside Judge Hatcher rushed forward, saying, "I'm Dr. Dorian Whitaker, Mr. Colfax. Let me come aboard and have a look at the man!" He fought his way forward and stepped onto the gangplank as it came down.

Brisbane shouted from where he and Lem were held. "Fact I ain't sheriff here no more doesn't change the facts. These people aboard my keelboat come up on me and Lem, got the drop on us and stole off to make free. They're all runaways!"

"At the courthouse, now! Everybody. We'll settle this confusion legally and rightfully," ordered Halverston, and the new sheriff and his deputies began escorting Isaac

Colfax, his sons, Daniel and the passengers from the flatboat.

The colorful red streamers still flapped in the wind.

CHAPTER TWENTY

ON TRIAL IN HANNIBAL

Hannibal's courtroom was filled. Daniel could feel Mrs. Shorr's eyes on him from as far back as twenty-four rows. She had not said a word to him, but he knew that she must be thinking that she had known all along "the boy will come to no good," as she'd told Judge Hatcher so often. Former Sheriff Brisbane and Lem sat at one table up front, alongside Hannibal's only lawyer whose name happened to be Lawyer, Lawyer Wilson. Folks called him Puddin'head behind his back. To their right, at another table up front, sat Mr. Colfax and his three sons. Daniel and all the workmen, crew, and passengers of the Excursion Line sat behind them. Every other seat and window-sill space spilled over with townspeople. Others stood just outside the open windows.

A black man in a fine suit stood up and announced, "All rise for the Honorable Judge William Halverston, presiding. This here is a Special Sessions of the Circuit Court of Hannibal, Missouri, this day of two December, 1852. Citizen Mr. Henry Brisbane versus Businessman and adventurer Mr. Isaac Colfax of the Colfax Excusion Tours. Plaintiff complaining is Mr. Brisbane, who says Mr. Colfax, defendant defending is a no-acount, low-down abolitionist running slaves off from hereabouts and having stolen Mr. Colfax's keelboat to do it with! Says Mr. Colfax is in possession of stolen goods, in the form of the boat and all these here black folks in your courtroom here today, judge."

193

"Billy? Is that you, Mr. Billy?" asked Daniel from his seat, realizing that the bailiff was indeed Old Billy.

"No talking from the floor in my courtroom!" said the colonel-turned-judge, his gavel coming down hard at Daniel's remark.

But Billy gave Daniel a smile and said, "You did us all proud, Daniel, landing a job on an excursion boat! Don't that beat all, judge? One of our town boys making good?"

Joe Grier and others at the window cheered this.

"You done well, too, Billy!"

Lawyer Wilson shot to his feet, shouting, "Objection, judge!"

"Agreed!" said Halverston. His voice was louder than his gavel this time. "Bailiff, you will carry on no more personal words with any of the defendants in the case."

"Yes sir, judge, but I know this boy wouldn't never be mixed up in no slave stealing or thieving of any kind, sir."

Another cheer followed this remark.

"Objection!" Lawyer Wilson again shouted. "This is highly prejudicial to Mr. Brisbane's case, your honor."

"Billy, no more remarks unless somebody wants to call you to the witness stand, do you understand?"

"I do, your honor, and I begs your pardon, sir, but there ain't a prejudicial bone in that boy's whole —."

"Bailiff! Do I have to remove you from these preceedings?"

"No sir, sorry sir." Under his breath, Billy muttered, "Now that Mr. Brisbane, now he's got all kinda prejudicial bones."

"State your case, Mr. Wilson," said the judge.

Wilson outlined a tale of how Brisbane, Lem and a posse of others had confiscated slaves they had caught and housed on the flatboat now docked at the landing, stolen slaves he had hoped to return to their rightful owners, as a man sworn to uphold the laws. Colfax, his sons, and the man Brisbane had laid low with a gunshot had snuck up on them in the middle of the night, shot the sheriff and near drowned Lem and had made off with the slaves, all of whom sat now in the courtroom before the judge.

Colfax, acting as his own lawyer, stood next and broke into laughter. "This is the most blatant, unsubstantiated pack of lies I have ever faced, but that's all right, for I have traveled the Far East and into India where I have faced tigers and snakes the size of a man's leg. This snake we have here...

"Objection!" shouted Wilson.

"Please refrain from name-calling, Mr. Colfax."

Colfax nodded but did not apologize. "The man is either deluded or a liar, judge."

"Objection!"

"Mr. Colfax."

"Sorry, Your Honor." Colfax simply repeated his story of why he and his passengers were touring the great cities of the South. Proud Hannibal citizens clapped at this. Lawyer Wilson objected to the clapping. When Colfax finished, he produced as exhibit A his ownership papers to the boat.

Both Judge Halverston and Wilson studied the papers, and Judge Halverston gaveled them into legitimacy, accepting them as real over Wilson's desire to send them out to the county seat for expert examination. Halverston refused. "Call your first witness," he told Wilson.

"I can't do that, judge."

"And why not?"

"Dred Scott case, your honor, a verdict being rendered from the Supreme Court, sir."

"What's the Dred Scott case got to do with this case?" Halverston glared down on Wilson.

Wilson pointed to the fifty black defendants in the case, saying, "These men and women are black, your honor."

"Is that a fact?"

"Whether free or slave, no black person in these here United States of America can hold citizenship. According to the Supreme Court, sir, and by extension, they can't sit in a witness box, since the highest court in the land says they have no rights as citizens."

Judge Halverston explained to everyone now confused by Lawyer Wilson: "I am aware of the case of this black man, Dred Scott, who took his fight all the way to the Supreme Court, Mr. Wilson. But I am not going to deny any man or woman, black or white, the right to speak up in my courtroom. This here is Missouri, not Washington, DC, Mr. Wilson." The judge threw it out to the people of Hannibal, saying, "Lawyer Wilson here wants me to deny these folks a trial because of some law passed in Washington. Folks, what say you?"

"This ain't Washington," agreed Judge Hatcher in the rear of the room.

"They got a right to a trial," said Joe Grier through the open window.

"Give 'em their day in court," said a rough-looking hill man. A shout of agreement followed this, and the trial continued.

"If we're to do it right, folks, it's up to Lawyer Wilson here to prove that Mr. Colfax is an abolitionist, and that these people are not freeborn sight-seeing tourists here, but some fifty runaway slaves!"

"Dress mighty fine for shoeless runaways," muttered Billy in the silence.

"Brisbane and Wilson have to prove beyond a shred of doubt that these people are guilty. That means these people are innocent and freeborn citizens of the North until somebody can show me unmistakable evidence to the contrary."

"I call Lem Deter to the stand, your honor," said Wilson, taking another tact. Lem told the same story as Brisbane, while Daniel began wondering how George might be doing at the doctor's office. Sissy and Daisy had stayed with George.

Colfax got his turn at Lem and the story that he and Brisbane had concocted. "Isn't it true, sir, that you and Sheriff Brisbane have in fact been running a scam all about these parts for years? Trapping up runaways in a keelboat like my boat out there at the landing, only to transport those runaways down to St. Louis? There to sell them on the auction block for your own gain, sir?"

"Sheriff and me wouldn't never do such a law-breaking thing."

"No, I suppose not. I have no more questions of this witness, your honor, but I would like to enter into evidence Exhibit B. My own birth certificate, showing I am who I state I am, sir, and with the bill of sale on the boat you already have, then the two documents support one another."

"Accepted into evidence," said the judge.

"Why don't we have some A, B and C's?" Lem asked Lawyer Wilson.

"Good question, your honor," said Colfax, pacing, "why hasn't Sheriff Brisbane produced his ownership papers on the boat, if it is indeed his?"

"Lost...lost in a storm," replied Brisane sullenly.

Halverston's eyes scanned from one document to the other, saying, "These look in order, gentlemen." Wilson rushed the bench to have a look, his face falling.

"Forgeries and lies!" shouted Brisane, getting to his feet and going for Colfax, shouting, "He stole them slaves and that excursion nonsense is a cover for the Underground Railroad!"

The mention of the freedom railway sent a hush over the crowd. Brisbane lashed out at Colfax, who expertly ducked and brought up a left to Brisbane's temple and a right to his stomach, sending Brisbane staggering back into the arms of Lem. Halverston gaveled and shouted for order, threatening to jail both men if they could not behave in a civil manner in his courtroom.

Colfax bowed and pleaded forgiveness. Brisbane scuttled back to his seat, grumbling. His eye began to swell.

Colfax turned to the people in the gallery and asked, "Have any of you ever seen slaves who dressed in the manner of my well-to-do patrons? Ever?"

"They don't look like no slaves I ever saw," said one man from the back.

"Don't talk or act like slaves," said the mill owner.

"We got a good man shot and likely dying over to your doctor's office, and we're looking at a huge delay in our schedule, judge, all on account of some mistaken identity," said Ichabod, who stood up from the crowd of Blacks on trial. "I speak for most here when I say, it's time we put this nonsense to rest. Will you run your judgeship's eyes across my freedom papers and tell me that I ain't who I say I am?"

"Let's see your papers, sir," said Halverston to Ichabod.

The white haired old man came forward just as Daisy and Sissy entered a side door, brought in by the new sheriff, Mr. Ken Morgan. When Daisy saw what Ichabod was up to, she pulled free and sassily walked to the bench as well, her parasol twirling. "You just have a good look at my papers, too, judge. Now, my boy's hurt real bad over there, and I brought you his papers, too. If he don't pull through, somebody's gonna pay."

"You'll make no threats here, Madam," the judge warned. Then he studied all three sets of papers, passing each in turn on to Wilson.

"Parson Palmer and Mrs. Hillock are right, your honor!" said Tom. He boldly stood to come forward. Mr. Fairfield's look of worry was mixed with a kind of pride as he saw Grady stand beside Tom. Grady added, "Your judgeship, I am Mr. Wileford, Charles Wileford the Third, and this man beside me is Mr. Ezeekiel Radcliff, and we, too, have the papers to prove it."

"Come forward Mr. Wileford the Third, Mr. Radcliff."

"Sound like a lot of exciting stories happen around here, but I got myself a piece of land up to Haymaker County in Michigan to get me back to before the cold comes on too harsh. I was freeborn in Michigan, you see, and my family has always held land there," Grady continued. He next spoke of his father and mother by name.

"Let me see those papers you mentioned, Mr. Wileford."

Tom spoke up next, telling about his home in Iowa.

"Let's see," began the judge, rubbing his chin thoughtfully, and asking, "Mr. Colfax, what does that put us at, Exhibit C for Mr. Palmer—Parson Palmer—D for Mrs. Hillock here, E for Mr. Wileford the Third and F for Mr. Radcliff?"

"Every one of my passengers has papers, your honor, so we could take up the whole alphabet and go 'round again."

"And the men working your crew?" asked the judge.

"All have bill of sale on 'em, and I got an arrangement with my slaves, your honor."

"Really, and what's that?"

"They work for their freedom. After six years of excursions, they can make up their minds to stay on and take a paycheck or go off free."

"They're all forgeries!" declared Brisbane, red-faced.

"Control your client, Mr. Wilson. As for the documents, I can find no evidence of forgeries, but entertaining the idea that I *have* been made a fool of, Mr. Brisbane, who in this room is so fine a forger that my eyes are deceived? Mr. Isaac Colfax? His sons? Daniel Webster Jackson?"

"That one that was shot, that's who! When I caught him bounty-hunting slaves himself, I found papers on him! Papers he made up."

"A bounty-hunting black man running slaves?" asked Halverston. "You want this court to believe that?"

"Ask Judge Hatcher!"

Halverston looked to the back of the room at his former opponent. "Judge, you got anything to add to Mr. Brisbane's allegations against the young man who was shot?"

Judge Hatcher bit his lip, shook his head and finally said, "No, I don't ever recollect such a character as former sheriff Brisbane speaks of."

"And Mr. Brisbane," continued Halverston, "are you calling me a fool? That I can be so readily and easily tricked by a black man with paper and pen? That a black man could outfox me, you, this entire assemblage, this entire town and county, sir?"

The crowd grumbled its mean agreement to this logic. Wilson got to his feet, saying, "My client didn't...doesn't meant to imply that you are a fool, your honor, no, nor that everyone in this room is a fool, no sir."

"Good!"

Daisy turned to the crowd and said, "I am Abigail Mosely Hillock. My beloved husband took the fever some three years ago, and my son, George, who is laying up in the doctor's office with that man's bullet in him, is the only-est thing I got left on this earth. Henry, my husband, was the best provider there could be, and he left just enough for comfort, and for a time, I feared spending any of it on this trip, but George, poor George, he wanted so to come on the excursion, so much I couldn't deny him. Now this...it were a grand trip till we hit Hannibal. Before this, we got to visit with some of our Southern relatives along the river, Uncle Rufus, Aunt Bess, but I'd have never stepped foot in Hannibal, Missouri had I known my poor baby George would be shot down like a dog by that man!" She ended with an angry glare and a pointing finger.

"All the rest of you who have papers, please submit them to my bailiff," Judge Halverston instructed. "Mr. Colfax, deliver up your papers on any crewmen who happen to be slaves, please. I can assure you, Mr. Wilson, every document will be examined thoroughly."

As this was done, Judge Halverston tested several more of the excursion people, asking about their histories, their homes. Then Lawyer Wilson asked if he could question one little girl who had come forward.

Colfax stiffened and Judge Halverston took in a deep breath but said, "That is your right, Mr. Wilson. Go ahead."

"What's your real pappy's name, child?" Wilson asked, smiling at the girl.

She shyly replied, "Benjamin McElroy and Meredith. Married 1829, but I didn't come along till six years later, after they give up hope of ever having me or any child, but Momma said no, that they had to have hope, and so here I be standing."

"What was your mother's maiden name?"

"Overton."

"Where were they married?"

"Keokuk."

Wilson looked from the small girl to the paper she'd produced, and it read the same. He then had a go at the five-year-old beside the girl, asking, "And Tad, where do you live?"

"Thaddeus is my name, not Tad. Only my pap can call me Tad. I was born in Cairo, Illinois, but we folks now live in Wisconsin."

Lawyer Wilson sat down, beaten. Brisbane conferred with him, whispering and furiously spitting in his ear. Brisbane knocked over a water pitcher and glasses at the table, shouting, "Judge, those slaves are mine! This nonsense has gone on long enough!"

"Yours, Brisbane? Why, when did you start holding slaves?" asked the judge.

"That is to say, they're my prisoners. I rustled them up from being runaways from over to Rantul County, where they run off from...from a fella named Blainy."

"And what Mr. Colfax here said about you running slaves to the auction block in St. Louis? That was all a fabrication?"

"Weren't no fabrication, it was an out and out lie, judge!"

"Even though there've been reports about you being seen in St. Louis selling off black folks on the auction block, Mr. Brisbane?" he asked.

"That's a bold-face lie, too, judge!"

"Well there is one way to find out if it's a lie or not, Mr. Brisbane," Halverston coolly replied, looking out over Daniel's head to someone in the back of the room. Daniel turned to see Mr. and Mrs. Blainy at the rear, alongside Judge Hatcher and Reverend Thornbush. Daniel's heart sank, and he saw that Daisy, Sissy, Ichabod and some of the others also saw their "rightful" owners as well. It appeared all was now lost.

"I have a Mr. Blainy in the courtroom, Mr. Brisbane. He's the man from Rantul County who came to me with a story of how some fella posing as a major from Louisiana managed to steal all of his slaves with a worthless check. I don't imagine you'd know who this here Major Splitshot might be, former Sheriff Brisbane?"

"Me, no...no sir," replied Brisbane.

Mrs. Blainy shouted, "That's the man, all right! He's the one flimflammed us out of our slaves!"

Mr. Blainy calmed his wife, and came forward. Judge Halverston said, "Mr. Blainy, I know you have experienced a major, major loss—no pun intended. But can you tell this court, sir, if any of these black people in the courtroom today are familiar to you, sir?"

A silence fell over the place like the hour before dawn. Daniel quaked in his skin. Then he heard Mr. Blainy plainly say, "No sir, not a one of them is mine. I'm afraid there's been a terrible mistake made, shooting at these people and holding these good folks up for trial."

Brisbane jumped to his feet, shouting, "Liar! You're a liar, Blainy! This ain't right! It's all turned around!"

"Sheriff, take Mr. Brisbane into custody. Hold him on the charge of attempted murder, lying to this court, and suspicion of slave-running for profit on some sort of backward, wrongway Underground Railroad."

"Yes, sir!" said the new sheriff with a smile.

"And take his partner there with him!"

The sheriff and his deputies marched Lem and Brisbane off, both men shouting their innocence. Brisbane kept yelling, "Have you all gone daft? Have you all gone soft on runaways?"

"These here proceedings are closed!" said Halverston, banging his gavel like a gunshot.

A roar went up among the crowd and the passengers of Colfax's Excursion Line.

CHAPTER TWENTY-ONE

SECRET CELEBRATIONS

Daniel rushed up to Old Billy, the two of them hugged and laughed. Daniel also took Colonel Halverston's hand and shook it, saying a warm thank you and asking, "What'll happen to Sheriff Brisbane and Lem?"

"Oh, no doubt we'll get Lem to tell us all we want to know about the former sheriff's little operation, and Brisbane will be behind bars for a long, long time, Daniel. Good to see you and your friends safe. Mrs. Halverston and I are proud of you, Daniel."

"So, son," said Billy, "what're you going to be doing now? You staying home in Hannibal where you belong, or you setting your sights for other horizons?"

Old Billy was like a father to Daniel, and Daniel loved the old man. "I'll be going North with the excursion and Mr. Fairfield, to learn the road, Billy. I got me a notion to help out folks like Mr. Ichabod, Miss Daisy and the others best I can."

Judge Halverston stopped at his chamber door, turned and whispered to Daniel, "Did you say Fairfield?"

"No sir, I mean, I meant Colfax."

"Is Colfax actually John Fairfield? You must tell me the truth, Daniel."

Daniel breathed deeply and nodded, saying, "He is."

"One and the same. He's known as one of the bravest men working a line on the Underground," whispered Halverston. "He's a legend, a living legend among people who know the operations of the road, among abolitionists North and South. He's wanted in every state south of the Mason-Dixon line. If he's ever caught this far south, he'll spend the rest of his days in a cell."

"I didn't know he was so popular, no sir," said Daniel.

Halverston shouted for Colfax, stopping him cold at the courthouse door. Colfax turned and said, "Yes, sir, judge?"

"Hannibal offers its sincerest regrets over this awful matter, and I'd like for you to be my guest at my home here in Hannibal. There're some special friends I'd like for you to meet."

"I don't know. My sons and I have a schedule to keep."

"Doctor says your passenger, Mr. Hillock, won't be capable of traveling for another day," the judge countered. "Besides, I know my wife, Amanda, would be angry if you left without her having the honor of meeting you. Say this evening?"

Mr. Fairfield smiled and replied, "I should be grateful to accept. But are you sure the lady would care to entertain a soldier of fortune such as myself?"

"Oh, but I know she would indeed, sir. My house, promptly at six, Mr. Colfax." The judge left.

In the next instant, Sissy rushed in, yelling the news that George was going to be all right. "His bleeding's stopped and all he needs now is rest."

"Lord praise the angels," said Daisy, holding firm to Ichabod, who supported her. Together they went off to visit George at the doctor's office.

"You sure your mind is set about going off with the excursion, Daniel?"

"I sure am, Mr. Billy."

"You done some mighty tall growing up these past few days, Daniel Webster Jackson."

"A might, yes, sir."

"War's a-coming, Daniel, sure as the river runs south, war's a-coming to this place."

"That's exactly what George said," replied Daniel as they walked out into the late afternoon sun.

"A boy like you, Daniel, at least you'll know where you stand. Most of the boys around Hannibal, white and black, are brought up such that they won't know what stand to take, and will likely take the wrong one when they do."

"Where're we going, Mr. Billy?" asked Daniel as he followed him.

"Why, you're my houseguest this evening, Daniel. I got myself a real smart place, right outside the judge's house, a thing they used to call the carriage house. Judge Hatcher spent a lot on fancy servants with French accents, on clothes and buggies, but that's all over now."

Daniel looked up at Mr. Billy's house, saying, "Why, it's grand, Mr. Billy! But I really ought to stop over to the doctor's to see George."

"Oh, he's got two women seeing after his every need. He ain't going nowheres," said Billy with a smile. "Besides, he'll have you all to himself tomorrow. They'll put him and you on that fancied up flatboat, and I won't never see you ever again."

"Why, that ain't so, Billy. I'll come to visit."

"You just come to visit tonight, young man," Billy stubbornly replied.

Daniel shook his head and said, "You think I won't ever be coming back to Hannibal because of the war, don't you, Mr. Billy?"

"'Cause of the war, 'cause of your work on the freedom road."

"It'll be mighty good learning from men like George Penrose, Mr. Fairfield and his sons, Billy."

"You run that line as long as you can, Daniel. This idea about using the excursion boat! It's the best notion. It's so brash, and I was so proud of those people, pulling it off the way they did. Think on it. I was proud of those people, my people!"

They stood before Old Billy's small but elegant white house with windows all around it. Daniel looked at the judge's large mansion alongside it, where the lights glowed warmly. "The judge has done scandalized the town over me, Daniel. The business of giving me my freedom papers, making me his bailiff and giving me the carriage house outright to live in, well...it don't set right with a lot of folks about here."

"Why don't you come away with us tomorrow, Billy, if'n you ain't comfortable here?"

"No, no, son. I can do a lot of good here so long as the colonel stays in office, don't you see?"

"You sure did a sight of good today in court for our side. Still, maybe you ought to take a trip up North, Mr. Billy, take some time away from Hannibal."

Billy tugged at his chin whiskers and said, "Daniel, maybe you're right. Judge Halverston might do a sight more good hereabouts if...if he didn't upset the locals over making me his bailiff. Maybe I ought to skee-daddle. See this here North I done sent so many others to see ahead of me. Maybe it is time I saw what's so all-fired good about up North."

"It'd be a grand time we'd have, Billy. You could tell stories along the way to all the passengers on the excursion."

Billy smiled wide at this. "I allow it might be best for the colonel's future as a judge in Hannibal, and so best for every single body in Hannibal, if'n I go."

Daniel nodded, understanding. "You're sure welcome to come, Mr. Billy. I know Mr. Fairfield wouldn't really charge you no money. He'd love to hear all about your days sending runaways north."

"Then it's settled. I'll pack my bags tonight and tell the colonel and his missus all about it. You know, they's going to give me a devilish fight over it."

"I'll go with you. Help them see your reasoning, Billy," Daniel assured him.

Old Billy and Daniel entered the mansion through the servant's entrance, following the long hallway to the front rooms where laughter and talk met them. When they saw that Mr. Fairfield was standing before a group of people and speaking openly about the Underground Railroad, Daniel couldn't believe his eyes or ears. Judge Halverston had settled in a chair beside his beautiful wife, Amanda, whose white evening gown took some of the attention off Mr. Fairfield. The room, filled with other men and women from the town, including Judge Hatcher and Reverend Thornbush, was gray with cigar smoke. Mr. Fairfield was in the middle of relating the tale of how the brave men of the Colfax keelboat boarded the steamboat *Walter Scott* as she sank to acquire clothes for themselves and the others to make the ruse in Hannibal work. Daniel could not believe his ears. For a moment, he wondered if Mr. John Fairfield might not be turning them all in, but Daniel relaxed when suddenly everyone clapped. Then Daniel saw Grady, Tom and Old Ichabod amble to the front of the room.

Judge Halverston stood and shook hands with the former Blainy slaves. His wife followed suit, and Old Billy whispered in Daniel's ear, "Just the night's entertainment, Daniel. Nothing to worry over. This'll bring more funds and converts to the cause of freedom."

"But there sits even Mr. and Mrs. Blainy," said Daniel. "I don't understand."

"They's all Hannibal folk, Daniel. All of them belong to the cause now, even some who've once held slaves.

They's all members of the secret Hannibal Abolition Society, all citizens of the territory who want to see an end to slavery in America."

"Daniel! Daniel Webster Jackson," Mr. Fairfield shouted over the assembly. "Ladies, gentlemen, this here is the brave young man I spoke about."

"The one who saved my life," Grady added with delight.

Ichabod ushered Daniel away from Billy and into the center of the room. "Saved the day, this boy did. More'n once."

"This is your day, son," Billy said with a smile, and Daniel realized only now that it had been Billy's job to get Daniel here for the surprise.

Daniel was wide-eyed as he realized that the people in the room weren't strangers at all. He shook hands with Mr. Barnes, the amiable owner of the land office. Daniel's mouth fell wide open when he shook hands with Dr. Horton, the new sheriff, the livery stable man, the owner of the grist mill, Jed Stamp the drygoods man, and Mr. Waverly the postal clerk.

"My-my-my word," stuttered Daniel. "I didn't know there was another abolitionist in the whole state besides the colonel and Old Billy."

"When did you start being one, Daniel?" asked Judge Hatcher.

Hatcher's quick, sparkling eyes met Daniel's. "Why, I've been against slavery all my life, Daniel. You needn't look so shocked."

"That's right, Daniel. There are a lot more of us than you might think. Tell us about your adventures, Daniel," said Dr. Horton, the man who had patched up George.

Jed Stamp added, "Most in our society couldn't get here on such short notice. But there are men all over Missouri who would have done all they could to help you and your friends, Daniel."

"Times have changed," added Judge Hatcher.

"How do you spot a friend?" Daniel asked. "I thought I couldn't trust nobody, not even Joe Grier, and for the longest time I felt awful bad about what I was doing, 'cause it's against the law, and I had to so often lie and go against what Mrs. Shorr always taught us in school, about what was right and proper."

A little amused laughter at this preceded what Colonel Halverston said. "You notice Mrs. Shorr is not one of us, Daniel. All of us in this room have lied, stolen and broken bad laws in order to help *fugitives* faced with a lifetime of slavery. Human bondage, even if it's protected by compromising lawmakers, Daniel, is against human dignity and the conscience of every good man."

Daniel looked a bit confused, and Ichabod simplified what Halverston meant by adding, "You followed your feelings, Daniel. You helped friends in need. You generally can't go wrong doing what your heart tells you is right."

Old Billy held his hands up and said, "Folks, I am here to make my own announcement. I intend at dawn to take the Colfax Excursion Tour upriver north to see what's so grand up there! I ask for your good wishes, and I mean to say my good-byes to you, one and all."

Old Billy's retirement speech was met with great cheers and congratulations.

⧗ ⧗ ⧗

The following day, Daniel and the Fairfield sons carried George out of the doctor's office and onto the keelboat. Old Billy, his valise packed, joined the excursion tour, and made a public show of paying his money to Mr. Isaac Colfax.

The band, and men, women, and children of Hannibal were assembled at the landing to say good-bye. The keelboat inched out to the center of the river amid cheers, streamers and waving. The flatboat's heading was once more due north.

"We're off for good this time," Daniel said to George, who now rested in what had been Sheriff Brisbane's bed. George had made a substantial recovery. Now he looked up at Daniel and smiled widely. His mother and Sissy stood at his bedside as well.

"Yeah, Daniel, but we'll be back again some day. Maybe when we return, Missouri will be a free state."

September 18, 1858

Daniel Webster Jackson's eyes moved over the scene, quickly taking in everything at the farmstead. He watched the mechanic, a white man, at work in the barn's loft, cursing at some pulley that didn't want to work properly. He watched a farmhand working on a fence at the chicken coop. The man stood hunched over; he was perhaps Old Billy's age when Daniel had first learned of the Underground Railroad six years ago. A woman came out of the coop with a basketful of eggs she'd gathered.

Daniel's trained eye measured off the steps the petite black woman took from the henhouse to the house. At the side door to the house, a large-handed, broad-faced woman at the door took the eggs from the younger woman and shooed her off. This woman, looking faintly like Daisy, stepped out onto the porch for a moment, and she stared right at Daniel as if she could see him where he lay in the tall Missouri grass, but she didn't see him so much as sense him.

Now twenty-one years old and a man, Daniel wondered if he had learned all his lessons well enough to succeed alone at what he meant to do here. He wished that Mr. Fairfield or George could have come along with him. But he was alone when he'd heard of the runaway slave named Jim. Heard the story in Hannibal, where he'd gone to visit Judge Halverston, who remained in office. Daniel's stopover was meant to be a one-nighter, but then Judge Halverston told him all about Jim. He'd run off from a Hannibal woman everyone knew as Widow Douglas. The widow had begun negotiations to sell Jim, and the man feared he'd be sold to Deep South, never to see his family again. He made a run at freedom. But before Judge Halverston or anyone working the local could help him, Jim had simply disappeared.

Daniel had been on the lookout for the runaway as he approached the colonel's former home. He wondered if any of the black people might know about Old Billy's underground cavern, and if Jim could be hidden there. With the papers he held, Daniel could take Jim, along with twenty others, right to Mr. Fairfield in Illinois. For all anyone would know, Daniel would not be stealing slaves and running them North, but returning runaways, since he and his dog, Sam, who lay beside him in the grass, were now runaway catchers by trade and reputation. George's original disguise as a runaway catcher had excellent results for Daniel, a white man, because it did not raise eyebrows.

He reached over now and lovingly patted Samuel. He thought of the last five years. Sam was as alert and as helpful as ever, and had become his dog. George, after several more years of working for Mr. Fairfield, went on to Canada and married Sissy. Ichabod and Daisy married and lived there too.

War continued to grow in liklihood with each passing day. The Underground Railroad continued as strong as ever. Mr. Fairfield ran the Colfax Steamer, billed as one of the greatest excursion tours on earth, twice a year, and he brought out seventy-five to one hundred slaves each year. Mr. Fairfield's sons had all married and had children of their own now, but they too continued to make the excursions into the South to bring out fugitive slaves. Old

Billy had passed away peacefully among his many friends and free slaves in Canada.

Back to the business at hand, Daniel now worked his way down to the dilapidated old quarters where Old Billy once made his home. Suddenly, a white haired old black man came around a tree and surprised Daniel. Their eyes met and he asked, "Who're you, young man? You looking for the massa?"

"My name is Daniel. I'm a...a friend...."

"A friend?"

"An agent."

"An agent? What kinda agent is you?"

"An agent on the road. I thought you might like to ship some cargo on the north line."

"Cargo? North line?"

"I'm heading for Canada and the North star."

The old man, who didn't look a lick like Billy up close, acted as if Daniel were talking in Portuguese. He squinted and looked off to where the main house still stood in disrepair. "Maybe you ought to come up to the big house, talk to my massa, son."

"I used to know the man who lived here once, a man who was Judge Halverston's slave, name of Old Billy."

"Judge Halverston don't own any slaves."

"He used to own this place and he had slaves, but Old Billy wasn't really no slave but a partner, and they trusted me. They showed me the passage, the cavern they used for their Underground Railroad station. Are you hiding this runaway named of Jim there now?"

"Jim who? I don't know nothing about no underground nothing, and I don't know nobody named Jim. You talking mighty crazy, mister."

Daniel pulled a beautiful gold watch from his pocket and dangled it on a chain. "You ever hear tell of Old Billy's chime watch? The one that saved his life once when he come up on some witches in Thatcher Woods?"

"You saying that's it? That's the watch Old Billy used?"

"You knew Old Billy, then?"

He shook his head and looked at the earth, "No, never had the pleasure, but I heard the story told over and over. Fact is, everyone in these parts tells stories 'bout Old Billy, how he everyday helped hundreds of his own out of slavery, a regular Moses he was."

"I worked with Old Billy on the last fifty people he helped to freedom, alongside Mr. John Fairfield and George Penny, and we done it with Judge Halverston's help."

"I hear Old Billy is living real good now in Canada."

"Then you'll trust me with Jim?"

"Come on, son. He's been cooped up below the big house for days. Not the massa, not nobody knows but me. We can't go trusting nobody, but since you know about the cavern and you're a friend of Old Billy's and John Fairfield's, then I gots to trust you."

The old man walked toward the meadow where Daniel's memory began to fill in the detail of the place. "I don't understand why Judge Halverston couldn't find Jim here. He knows about the cavern and he's a friend, like I am."

"You don't know how bad it's got hereabouts, that's all. Some lynching and lesson-making going on, son. A man like the judge can't be too careful these days, 'cause everyone knows he cares 'bout us slaves. Some folks calling him names over it."

"There's going to come a mighty big reckoning over slavery. I'm certain," said Daniel.

THE END

Postscript:

In 1861 The War Between The States erupted over the issues of slavery and states' rights.